THE
BLACKBURN
ROVERS
MISCELLANY

HARRY BERRY

To Archie & Izaak

First published in 2012 by

The History Press
The Mill, Brimscombe Port
Stroud, Gloucestershire, GL5 2QG
www.thehistorypress.co.uk

British Library Cataloguing in Publication Data.
A catalogue record for this book is available from the British Library.

ISBN 978 0 7524 6399 5

Typesetting and origination by The History Press
Printed in Great Britain

INTRODUCTION

I t is over sixty years since I started following the Rovers, which was the club of my grandfather. My son, Karl, has been attending matches with me for 37 years, my nephew, Andrew Smith, for almost as long. My grandson, Archie, attended his first game when aged three, my youngest grandson, Izaak, is keen to start. We bleed blue and white in our family. The recent events at the club have made it harder to be a Blackburn Rovers supporter than at any time I can remember. I have had a season ticket since 1960, when I left school, but this year was the first time that I seriously contemplated not renewing it. I am not unique in my feelings. Many Rovers supporters of long standing have taken the decision to withhold their support from the club that they love. Supporters as old as me have lived through similar circumstances. In 1960, the year that they reached the final of the FA Cup, the club had an average gate of 27,299. There was a widespread dissatisfaction over the distribution of the cup final tickets, compounded by the fact that it was well known that the players were dealing openly in them. The following year the average attendance was 19,343, the season after 15,906. Those who stayed away never came back. It took the arrival of Jack Walker and the winning of the Premiership to build the gates back to the levels of the 1950s. Yet in 1960 the depth of feeling was not as great as it currently is. Those like myself for whom the club has been a huge part of our lives, fear the future. Each wrong step the club takes reduces the core support and ensures that more and more Blackburn people start catalogue shopping for a favourite club on Sky, and never return to the fortnightly pilgrimage to Ewood Park.

This has been a great club that has achieved more than any small town has a right to expect. A galaxy of truly great players has pulled on the blue and white. In my childhood the club had Ronnie Clayton and Bryan Douglas, players who still rank in the top five all-time great players of the Rovers. It was a privilege as well as an education to watch the way they influenced games in their different ways. In 1959 the club won the FA Youth Cup with three players, Keith Newton, Mike England and Fred Pickering, who would have graced any team in the world. Later came Alan Shearer, about whom any comment would be superfluous and Henning Berg, the most technically gifted defender who has ever worn the blue and white. Even when the club could not sustain the impetus of the Jack Walker years there were still Brad Friedel and Tugay, players of ability way beyond the ordinary. It has been gratifying to have these great players but the Blackburn crowd has never been one to only welcome the stars. Hard work and commitment are the qualities demanded above all and few players who display these facets are ever ill-received at Ewood. Demonstrative of this is that by far the most popular player of the modern age is Simon Garner, a character, a loyal club man, a good goalscorer and a man whose heart is divided into blue and white halves even if his training methods would not find their way into any text book. Yet what makes Blackburn Rovers truly unique is that the crowd never fail to acknowledge their debt to Jack Walker, who brought success to the club beyond the realms of anything the most optimistic fan could have dreamed of.

PRIMORDIAL ROVERS

The history books are quite clear that Blackburn Rovers FC was formed on 5 November 1875, at a meeting at the St Leger Hotel. Yet a team called Blackburn Rovers had preceded them. Ten years before this climactic date, sport in the town was limited to cricket and athletics in the summer and the occasional game of rugby in the winter. However, Albert Hornby had started working at his father's mill, Brookhouse, and decided to organise football games for his workers. He found them adept and formed his own team to provide the opposition – they came from the well-heeled in town and called themselves the Rovers. In addition to Hornby, who later played cricket and rugby for England, there were his brothers Harry and Cecil, Joseph Law, Arthur Appleby, Hugh Pickering and William Baynes. The rest have been obscured by time and those named are only remembered because of the subsequent memories of Joseph Law, a local bookseller. Harry Hornby was later to become Sir Harry, after public service that included 24 years in Parliament (without making a maiden speech) and two spells as Mayor of Blackburn. His brother Cecil played the odd cricket game for Lancashire, but became a professional soldier, serving with distinction in the Zulu and Boer Wars. Appleby, the son of an Enfield mill owner, played for a long time for Lancashire and was described by Albert Hornby as 'a good left-arm trundler.' Pickering was a successful brush maker in the town and Baynes, the first pupil to enrol at Blackburn Grammar School when it was reopened, became a man of the cloth, ending his days in Herefordshire. Strangely as proof of some egalitarianism, the names of the Brookhouse team have survived.

THOUGHTS ON BLACKBURN

'Blackburn is a proud, working-class area, Blackburn Rovers is their outlet. They live in rows of houses with no gardens and they don't like it when we play badly.'

Ryan Nelsen

'It always seems to be pitch dark by 3.30 in Blackburn and if you want to go shopping there is nothing to buy and there's no decent language school.'

Stéphane Henchoz

'It's a shithole.'

Lucas Neill

'When you are driving through Blackburn, shut your eyes. This is no disrespect to Blackburn but see beyond it. This place is changing.'

Kenny Dalglish's advice to Kevin Gallacher

'I wouldn't want to live in Blackburn. The place is lovely and I'm not saying the fans would be trouble but I know if I walked into a fish and chip shop in Blackburn I'd get noticed.'

Ryan Nelsen

'The town is unhealthy. Even to natives the climate is very trying. I always regard health as the greatest wealth. I refuse to sacrifice my family on the altar of mammon.'

Archie Kyle explaining his decision to flee Blackburn in the summer of 1909

A MAN OF FEW PUBLIC WORDS

In his 8 glorious seasons with the club, the much-loved Tugay only spoke to the press once, in his first season. After that he refused all interviews, even with the club's own radio station. When he finally retired in May 2009, the final game of the season was set aside to celebrate his huge contribution to the club and his unique bond with the fans. Tugay masks were distributed and the fans special chant, 'You're my Turkish Delight', was sung throughout. At the end Tugay finally spoke, 'I love you and I'll miss you,' and then handed the microphone back to the interviewer.

CORNER SHOPS

When the Rovers reached the final of the FA Cup in 1960 there was some conjecture over whether the club would bring back their much loved English international, Bill Eckersley, for a swansong to his illustrious career. The management was obviously unaffected by sentiment and the regular occupant of the number three shirt, Dave Whelan, played although he might have been better to have opted out since he broke his leg during the game, an injury that blighted his career. Both men are also connected by corner shops.

Whelan started a business career with a corner shop in Mill Hill, moved on to a stall in Wigan market, built up a supermarket chain that he sold to the Morrisons organisation and used the proceeds to build up the JJB sports chain. Eventually he turned it into a public company, making him one of the richest men in the United Kingdom. With his wealth he indulged his passion for sport and at one time owned

Wigan Athletic, Wigan Rugby League Club and Orrell Rugby Union Club. Ultimately he concentrated on the football club and guided them into the Premier League.

Bill Eckersley had for a time, a small grocery and confectionery shop not a hundred yards from Ewood Park. It was a small terraced building with a shop window either side of a central doorway. On one particular day Eckersley had two tins of peas in the left showcase and his collection of English caps in the right one. Derek Dougan, who was injured at the time, strolled past with a friend on his way to watch the reserves. He stopped at Eckersley's shop, shook his head and observed, 'Bill's not really got the hang of retailing, has he?' Eckersley's collection of caps were almost consumed by fire at the house in 1958 when an overturned paraffin stove caused a fire that was put out by Bill Marlow, a passing policeman.

In that FA Cup final of 1960, the Rovers team contained three men who were shopkeepers, John Bray (sweet shop), Ronnie Clayton (newsagent) and Dave Whelan (grocer).

PRACTICAL JOKERS

Every club has its practical jokers but there have seldom been two such outrageous exponents at one club at the same time as the Rovers possessed in the 1950s, with Bill Eckersley and Jack Campbell. They appeared to be driven to fresh excesses in an endeavour to surpass each other but it was Eckersley who finally won the contest conclusively. When the team were staying overnight in a hotel, he shinned down the drainpipe into Campbell's room and, disguised by a balaclava, relieved Campbell of his watch and wallet.

Campbell came back to Ewood Park for an old boys' reunion, not long before his death at his home in Spain. A sprightly pensioner, his last act on the Ewood turf was to attempt to stick the point of his umbrella up the rear of the Wolverhampton mascot.

SOME CAME RUNNING

The introduction of substitutes took football into places where there was no etiquette as to how these men behaved. Forced to await a call to action, it did not escape their team-mates' notice that certain individuals were forever trying to catch the manager's eye. Even worse were the ones who stripped off the minute the trainer was allowed on the field. No such charge could be levelled at Eamonn Rogers, a somewhat laid-back young man with an amiable disposition who was badly misrepresented by the press as a consequence of a series of confrontations with the management. Eddie Quigley, the Rovers manager, had experience of how cold it can get in Blackburn and as a player had been a master at conserving his energy. He therefore ordered a massive sleeping bag to keep the substitute warm, rather than have him expending his strength running up the touchline. In one particular game he suddenly caught the referee's eye so that he could introduce Rogers as a substitute. Unfortunately he had not communicated his intention to the player, who remained swathed in the cocoon that was his sleeping bag, with only the point of his nose on display. Quigley had to bend down to his eye level to inform him of the action required, and this appeared to flummox the player, giving rise to the rumour that he had in fact been asleep. Certainly his efforts to remove the bag were laborious – Harry Houdini used to escape from chains and a straitjacket in considerably less time than it took Rogers to discard his sleeping bag! When he was finally revealed he was wearing a track suit. Even when this was discarded no blue and white shirt could be seen and not until two sweaters had been removed did he appear ready to take the field. Except that he was not wearing his boots, which he appeared to have somehow misplaced and were only located after a frantic search of the dugout.

NICKNAMES

Comparatively few players acquire original nicknames. The majority involve a mangling of their name but occasionally there are a few that transcend the normal. Here are a few.

Cheyenne	Derek Dougan
The Tank	John Bray
Braveheart	Colin Hendry
The Bull of the Bosphorus	Hakan Şükür
Woody	Alf Woolfall
Dino	Don Martin
Chip	Tom Briercliffe
Basil	Mick Rathbone
Pepper	Ernest Bracegirdle
Tiny	John Joyce/Martin Taylor
Pinkie	Eddie Latheron
Nudger	Jack Campbell
Skimmy	Jack Southworth
Iron Man	Willie Kelly
Killer	Glenn Keeley

Tex	Terry Eccles
Noddy	Ally MacLeod
Spider	Dave Helliwell
Ciccio	Corrado Grabbi
Mbazo (The Axe)	Aaron Mokoena
Tinker	William Davies

Some require explanation. 'Woody' was bestowed upon an early goalkeeper, Alf Woolfall, because of his occupation as a cabinet maker; 'Tinker' was also an occupational association; 'Noddy' arose because of the peculiar action of MacLeod's head when he ran and Derek Dougan was nicknamed when he shaved his head like the TV character Cheyenne (Clint Walker). It promoted some amusement when Bill Fryer, the *Daily Express* columnist remarked that, 'if he wore Cheyenne's hat he would look like a knitting needle.' Despite the inventiveness of fans, nicknames seldom become commonly accepted. When the flying Greek winger George Donis was signed, the local paper assured the fans that in Athens he was nicknamed the 'Greek Greyhound'. No one swallowed the story.

FOR SOME IT'S EASY

Making a career in football can be easy, but it can also be tortuous. As an illustration the case of Bill Eckersley can be compared with that of Albert Clarke. In the winter of 1947 Eckersley was newly demobbed from the army and had returned to his native Southport, where he found work driving a grocery delivery van. He went back to his local junior club, High Park, and played his first game for them, making the reacquaintance of a wing-half named Johnny Fairhurst.

Fairhurst had been on amateur terms with the Rovers since 1938 but had just turned 29 and had played just three times for the reserves. Another invitation to play for the Rovers' A team was not about to further his career, as his wife pointed out, and he decided to end his association with the Rovers. Unable to contact anyone at the club he asked Eckersley if he would take his place. The ever-amiable Eckersley agreed, the Rovers let him play and were so impressed he was offered terms immediately. Little did they realise that they were signing the man who would quickly become their left-back and captain and an England partner for Alf Ramsey.

Albert Clarke had burning ambitions to become a footballer and escape the hardships of the north-east of the mid-1930s. He and a friend packed a change of clothing in a brown paper bag and with little money set off walking and hitchhiking to Torquay, a club where they thought they had the best chance of being given a start. They made the 400-mile journey and talked Torquay into giving them a trial, at the end of which they were both signed, freeing them of the necessity of retracing their steps to the north-east. Four years later Clarke joined the Rovers, scored 21 goals in his first season and helped the club gain promotion to the First Division. Sadly his promising career was cut short as he died on the beaches in Normandy, serving with the Devon Regiment.

YOUNGEST SCORERS

Thomas Campbell	15y 317d	26 March 1881
Jimmy Haydock	17y 71d	27 September 1890
Jimmy Brown	17y 107d	15 November 1879
John Byrom	17y 134d	9 December 1961

Stuart Metcalfe	17y 340d	11 September 1968
Peter Dobing	17y 344d	10 November 1956
Billy Dunning	18y 20d	5 December 1970
Paul Round	18y 63d	26 March 1977
Malcolm Darling	18y 132d	13 November 1965
Tony Diamond	18y 161d	31 January 1987
Mark Patterson	18y 194d	4 December 1983
Damien Duff	18y 251d	8 November 1997
Terry Eccles	18y 313d	9 January 1971
George Jones	18y 330d	13 March 1964
Roy Vernon	18y 370d	10 March 1956
Simon Garner	18y 345d	3 November 1978
Ben Anderson	18y 353d	6 February 1965
David Dunn	19y 41d	6 February 1999
Gerry McDonald	19y 64d	14 August 1971
David Bradford	19y 66d	26 April 1972
Bob Crompton	19y 98d	2 January 1899

THE YOUNGEST DEBUTANTS

Thomas Campbell	15y 317d	26 March 1881
Harry Dennison*	16 y 155d	8 April 1911
Ronnie Clayton	16y 263d	25 April 1951
Jimmy Haydock	17y 71d	27 September 1890
Jimmy Brown	17y 79d	15 October 1879
Doc Greenwood	17y 80d	19 January 1878
John Byrom	17y 106d	11 November 1961
Adam Henley	17y 158d	19 November 2011
Bob Crompton	17y 196d	10 April 1897
Stuart Metcalfe	17y 203d	27 April 1968
Mick Wood	17y 212d	21 January 1970

Phil Jones	17y 213d	22 September 2009
Harry McShane	17y 261d	25 December 1937
Neil Wilkinson	17y 269d	11 November 1972
Paul Bradshaw	17y 295d	17 February 1974
Dewi Atherton	17y 296d	28 April 1969
Jay McEveley	17y 298d	6 November 2002
Peter Dobing	17y 302d	29 September 1956
Alan Bean	17y 303d	15 November 1952
Mike England	17y 305d	3 October 1959
Mick Salmon	17y 305d	15 May 1982
Glenn Wright	17y 324d	16 April 1974
Aaron Doran	17y 333d	11 April 2009
Terry Eccles	17y 335d	31 January 1970
Billy Dunning	17y 364d	14 November 1970

* Harry Dennison was actually selected for the reserves when still a pupil at Blackburn Grammar School. Unfortunately no-one told the doorman, who refused him admission to the dressing room.

OLDEST PLAYERS

Bob Crompton	40y 150d	23 February 1920
Dickie Bond	39y 39d	22 January 1923
Tugay	38y 273d	24 May 2009
Mark Hughes	38y 191d	11 May 2002
Kevin Moran	38y 8d	7 May 1994
Bobby Langton	37y 255d	21 April 1956
Arnold Whiteside	37y 166d	21 April 1949
Syd Puddefoot	37y 126d	20 February 1932

Brad Friedel	36y 356d	13 May 2008
Craig Short	36y 316d	7 May 2005
Youri Djorkaeff	36y 228d	23 October 2004
Herbert Jones	36y 189d	11 March 1933
Ronnie Sewell	36y 117d	13 November 1926
Michel Salgado	36y 50d	11 December 2011
Dave Wagstaffe	35y 343d	14 March 1979
Bob Pryde	35y 338d	23 April 1949
Alan Ainscow	35y 302	13 May 1989
Ossie Ardiles	35y 288d	18 May 1988
Johnny McIntyre	35y 237d	3 December 1927
Len Butt	35y 155d	28 January 1946
Reg Elvy	35y 147d	21 April 1956

DID YOU KNOW?

Robert Crompton is always described as being 'Blackburn through and through', yet his father and generations of Cromptons before him, were born in Darwen.

A reserve goalkeeper, Charles Saer, was the first president of the PFA. A Welshman who made his home in Fleetwood, he became a teacher in the town where a primary school is named after him.

In 2002, when on holiday in South Africa, Roy Wegerle qualified for the Alfred Dunhill golf championship, which was a European Tour event.

Martin Andresen was a proficient bridge player who competed in the North American Bridge Championship.

Andy McEvoy, one of Rovers' greatest goalscorers, was honoured posthumously when a competition in Ireland was named the Wicklow and District Andy McEvoy Premier League.

PILLARS OF SOCIETY

Five Rovers players who became policemen:

James Carter
Robert McFarlane
Thomas Baxter
Martin Fowler
Robert Thompson

Jack Fairbrother, a wartime guest, was a policeman in Blackburn.

And six who became school teachers:

William Townley
Jimmy Haydock
Harry Dennison
Norman Christie
Peter Vause
Bill Holmes

Percy Fish, who played for the club during the First World War, became a headmaster in Blackburn.

THE CRADLE OF LANCASHIRE

The Lancashire Football Association was formed in 1878 and between 1879 and 1890 selected teams for county games, which were designed to raise funds for the association. The cream of Lancashire players (including the imported Scots) turned out during this golden era, which terminated when the formation of the Football League caused clubs to refuse to co-operate. The identity of the power brokers of Lancashire football can be seen in the following table of county representatives per club:

Blackburn Rovers	26
Bolton Wanderers	24
Accrington	22
Darwen	21
Blackburn Olympic	19
Turton	14
Preston North End	13
Church	13
Burnley	6
Everton	6
Newton Heath	1

YES MR WENGER, THEY DID PLAY RUGBY

Although they were formed as an Association Football club, the Rovers had one experience of playing rugby. On 16 February 1878 they travelled to Penwortham to take on Preston Rovers. Harry Greenwood had experience of the game at Malvern and had been playing with the newly formed town rugby union team. He brought along his back partner, Roger Howorth, who later became the Rovers goalkeeper. Walter Duckworth and Jack Baldwin played at three-quarter, Fred Hargreaves played scrum half and partnering him the club brought in a skill player who knew how to play rugby: Joseph Bulcock, a Clitheroe dentist. Tom Dean, John Lewis and Tom Lonsdale formed the front row. Robert Howard and John Lightbourne, the son of a Scottish doctor, were brought in from rugby clubs and the line-up was completed by William Standing and T.J. Syckelmore (who had rugby experience from his undergraduate days in Cambridge). Despite playing two men understrength, Blackburn actually scored first when they kicked a goal, although their opponents disputed the score being awarded. Thereafter Blackburn surrendered by 5 tries, 2 touchdowns and 5 dead balls and it was said, 'they did not seem at home with the rugby game.' If it was any consolation the newly formed Blackburn town team had played the same opposition on 28 October 1877 and lost by 2 goals, 4 tries, 3 dead balls and 2 touchdowns to a touchdown.

STRANGERS IN GREEN

In these days of multiple substitutes it is unusual for an outfield player to have to take over in goal, although ex-Rovers player Robbie Savage did for Derby in 2010, following an injury and a sending-off in the same game. Once, though, it was a fact of football life and teams generally had one player who had spent some time during training trying his hand at goalkeeping. It was common knowledge in Blackburn that Bill Eckersley fancied his chances with the gloves on and regularly went in goal during training. It was a lot of effort for 6 minutes of deputising, although Eckersley enjoyed it enormously, prowling around the penalty area in Harry Leyland's huge, green jersey which came down to his knees. On one occasion he almost started a game in goal. During the warm-up the Ewood fans were alarmed when Harry Leyland was left flat out. The manager, Johnny Carey, formulated a plan. Eckersley would start the game in goal and the club would play with ten men, until the arrival of the third team goalkeeper, Alan Ross, who was playing with the A team in Darwen. Fortunately Leyland came round without any concussion and was able to start.

Nobody has been called into the breach more often than the international wing-half, Bill Bradshaw, who went into goal no less than eight times (the penalty of playing with the recklessly courageous Alf Robinson). Jock Hutton even managed to save a penalty when he went in goal against Bolton, although the ball was hit straight at him. The last outfield player to go in goal was Andy Kennedy, who also had the longest spell, coming on after a minute at Exeter. After that the presence of substitute goalkeepers on the bench have lessened the trauma (and the excitement) when a goalkeeper needs to be replaced during the game.

SPOT ON

Subjectivity is the life blood of football but when it comes to penalties the figures speak for themselves.

Player	Total	Scored	Saved	Missed	Scored from rebound	Tapped forward
Billy Bradshaw	28	22	4	2		
Bryan Douglas	28	18	5	3	1	1
Bill Eckersley	25	18	1	5	1	
Bobby Langton	22	18	2	2		
Alan Shearer	20	18	1		1	
David Dunn	20	17	3			
Bill Imrie	15	12	1	2		
Simon Barker	15	13	1	1		
Howard Gayle	15	10	2	2	1	
Mike Harrison	14	13	1			
Jack Bruton	14	9	2	3		
Tony Field	14	12	1	1		
Ted Harper	12	10		2		
Kevin Hird	12	10	2			
Peter Dobing	11	8	3			
Kevin Stonehouse	11	10	1			

One category that needs explanation is the 'tapped forward' column. In a League Cup tie on an Ewood Park that was ankle-deep in mud, Bryan Douglas merely tapped the penalty he was taking, so that Mike Ferguson could run on and dribble the ball into the net. Mike Harrison was perhaps the best Rovers penalty-taker of all time, yet he placed every penalty he took in the same place, along the ground just inside the goalkeeper's right-hand post. Once in the last game of a season, at Fulham, Kevin Hird demonstrated a surprising ignorance of the rules of the game. His penalty kick was saved by the goalkeeper but bounced straight back to him. Under the impression that he could not touch the ball again he screamed for a team-mate to come and kick it, allowing Fulham an unexpected reprieve.

CORDON BLEU

The rapid success of the club in the 1880s placed many of the working men in the team in situations outside of their upbringing. English cup successes made it necessary to attend social functions at large London hotels, where the players struggled to adapt to their surroundings. When a waiter brought 'Tot' Strachan a bowl of rose water to clean his fingers, the little inside forward drank it. Told of his faux pas, he said nonchalantly, 'I've had woss soup, mony a time.'

The young full-back, Jim Ward, was a well known trencher man who regularly tucked away a huge plate of potatoes before a meal. His career actually ended when he was injured trying to jump over a table after over indulging himself with both knife and fork and pint pot. When the goalkeeper, Herbie Arthur, who came from a social background a couple of steps up from Ward, decided to sample the lobster salad, he soon persuaded Ward to accompany him on what for Ward was uncharted, culinary territory. When the dish arrived it clearly disappointed the eager 'foodie' – 'Wey, it's nobbutt rapput, mate.'

WHEN YOU NEED A MAN USED TO SAVING, IT DOES NO HARM TO HAVE TWO

In 1888 the Rovers players were relaxing near the end of the season at Derwentwater, in the Lake District. Some of the swimmers in the party went out in a rowing boat and used it as a landing stage as they dived in and swam around. Billy Almond and Joe Beverley, who were unable to swim, sat on the end of the bathing board, dangling their legs in the water. It was hot and Almond, believing the water to be 3 or 4ft deep, slid off the board. He realised his error when he kept descending – the depth was about 12ft. Coming to the surface he had the presence of mind to shout to those on the boat, one of whom, Billy Townley, sized-up the situation immediately. Grabbing the oar he flung it in Almond's direction, with unerring accuracy. It struck him on the head, dazing him and causing him to go under again. Tragedy was averted by the two goalkeepers in the party, Herbie Arthur, who was the star of the Blackburn Swimming Club, and Alf Woolfall. They jumped straight in and brought Almond to the surface, saving his life. It was subsequently pointed out, with some irony, that they had not sought the reward paid out by the Royal Humane Society for such acts of rescue. It was also questioned as to why Townley did not adopt a more constructive role in the events because he had been boasting about having swum 'two lengths of the Blackburn slipper baths.'

THE TWENTY-FIVE

There can be few subjects that have commanded so many column inches as the Premier League's introduction of a registration scheme for eligible players, brought in for the 2010/11 season. Seldom can a topic have produced so many warnings of the consequences that were totally wrong. Tales of experienced players being frozen out proved incorrect and in the end the press were hard pushed to find more than a handful of players who might have been expected to have been registered but weren't, and most of these were found to be recovering from long-term injuries. Most of the dire warnings stemmed from a misunderstanding of the rules which, while mostly basic, have some complexities.

The first rule is that a club can register up to twenty-five players (this is a maximum number not a minimum) aged 21 or over (on 1 January) of whom eight have spent three years up to the age of 19 at a recognised English or Welsh club. If a club falls short of the required number of English-trained players, then the twenty-five places available for registration is reduced by the number by which they fall short.

Players under 21 are not included in the registration but can still be played in the Premier League.

If a club does not register its full complement of 25 players (or such lower number calculated after consideration of the qualifying trained players) any player aged over 21 who is signed with the club will automatically be added to the registered list.

Revision of the registered list occurs twice a season, immediately after the close of the transfer window. Players can be added outside of the registration dates if the club has not reached its maximum registration number calculated as above and the players were free agents with no contract with any club. Places cannot be freed up by any loan move that takes the player away from the club and a returning player automatically resumes his registration place.

So with all these new rules, on 1 September 2010 the club registered the following players:

Goalkeepers – Robinson, Bunn, Fielding, Brown
Defenders – Salgado, Givet, Samba, Nelsen, Chimbonda
Midfielders – Emerton, E.H. Diouf, Dunn, Pedersen, Olsson, Andrews, Grella, N'Zonzi
Attackers – Kalinić, M.B. Diouf, Benjani, Roberts

The club registered 21 players although they could have registered 25 since they had eight qualifying players – the four goalkeepers, Dunn, Andrews, Olsson and Roberts. Ironically four of these were international players with countries other than England – Brown (Wales), Andrews (Republic of Ireland), Olsson (Sweden), Roberts (Grenada). There was some conjecture why the club registered a fourth goalkeeper and Jason Roberts who had been informed that he would not play for the club and had not been allocated a squad number but under the rules they would have been automatically added even if they had not been included in the club's submission.

In November the club signed the free agent Herold Goulon, increasing their registered number to 22. In the January transfer window El Hadji Diouf and Pascal Chimbonda left but the squad was increased by new signings Roque Santa Cruz, Jermaine Jones and Mauro Formica. The other new signing, Rubén Rochina, did not require registration as he was under 21.

BY THE NUMBERS

Squad numbers still continue to attract a surprising amount of interest among the fans, although as they are issued in the close season it is perhaps a case of nothing else to talk about.

When the Premier League introduced them in August 1993 the Rovers allocated the numbers as follows:

1   Bobby Mimms
2   David May
3   Alan Wright
4   Tim Sherwood
5   Colin Hendry
6   Graeme Le Saux
7   Stuart Ripley
8   Kevin Gallacher
9   Alan Shearer
10 Mike Newell
11 Jason Wilcox
12 Nicky Marker
13 Matt Dickins
14 Lee Makel
15 Richard Brown
16 Tony Dobson
17 Patrik Andersson
18 Andy Morrison
19 Simon Ireland
20 Henning Berg
21 Kevin Moran
22 Mark Atkins

The obvious iconic and definitive numbers would be the five of Colin Hendry and the nine of Alan Shearer. Strangely the other numbers that evoke memories would probably be the seven and eleven of the wide men, Stuart Ripley and Jason Wilcox.

The unlucky number thirteen was given the reserve goalkeeper Matt Dickins, who had a subsequent career in keeping with the award. The number has continued to be handed to the reserve goalkeeper with the following having had to cope with the curse associated with it: Frank Talia, Bobby Mimms, Shay Given, John Filan, Alan Kelly, Peter Enckelman and Mark Bunn. If Dickins was proof of the superstition there appears to be ample rebuttal in the success of Shay Given and John Filan. On the other hand Enckelman is now legendary for his gaffes and Talia was nominated substitute on 28 occasions with the club and never played a single minute of first-team football. Then there is the real exception to the rule. In 2007 the thirteen was assigned to centre-back, Zurab Khizanishvili, though whether that was due to his lack of superstitious belief or the fact that the number has a different significance in Georgia, is not known.

Following Alan Shearer in the number nine shirt was always going to be a tall order but for a time the standard fell little with Chris Sutton moving into the shirt. From then on, however, it was downhill. How do you quantify the gap in class from Shearer/Sutton to Ashley Ward? Then came Kaba Diawara, an ageing Mark Hughes, Marcus Bent, Andy Cole, Jon Stead, Shefki Kuqi, Shabani Nonda, Roque Santa Cruz, Jason Roberts, Niko Kalinić and Anthony Modeste. Santa Cruz had one season playing at the standard set by the original number nine, Cole is remembered with affection for his winning goal in the Worthington Cup final and Jon Stead scored the goals that kept the club in the Premier League, but these have been scarce highlights in a number that now represents the fans' disillusionment. There was an amusing attempt by Jason Roberts, who displayed a politician's grasp of actuality, to claim that his scoring record compared with the best. To achieve this he calculated the ratio of goals scored against the games he had started, arguing that substitute games did not count. However, he failed to deduct from his goals scored the high proportion that were obtained when he came on as substitute. For the record, the minutes per goal of the wearers of the number nine (discounting Mark Hughes who played in midfield) are as follows: Shearer (114), Sutton (229), Ward (394), Diawara (279), Bent (239), Cole (224), Stead (377), Kuqi (256), Nonda (265), Santa Cruz (219), Roberts (303), Kalinić (249), Modeste (386 minutes played – no goal scored). There can be only one qualification in these figures, for Sutton, who spent some time as a central defender.

On the other hand the number one has never represented anything other than excellence. From Tim Flowers and John Filan through to Brad Friedel and Paul Robinson, the jersey has always been in safe hands.

In the early days managers had to take care not to offend players who would be upset by not having a number in the one to eleven range. That said, Morten Gamst Pedersen has been a first-team regular for six years, but has always worn the number twelve. The highest number of shirt ever allocated at the Rovers, is the 45 given to Bryan Hodge, but it never saw first-team action. Occasionally the shirt number can be used to make a point. In the summer of 2010 the relationship between Sam Allardyce and Jason Roberts descended to the point where there appeared no way forward. Allardyce made it clear that he did not intend to select the player again and therefore did not give him a shirt number. Three months later he was forced to relent and indeed two months after that it was Allardyce, and not Roberts, who left the club.

FOREIGN LEGION

Most sources attribute Bob Priday, the South African left winger, as being the club's first foreign player, when he was signed from Liverpool in March 1949. However, during the First World War the club had played a local wing-half named Albert Marinus 'Bert' Proos, who was born in Holland in about 1893. His parents, Marinus and Maria, had come to Blackburn in about 1898 and Marinus worked as a carpenter. The children were educated in Blackburn and their descendants still live in the area.

What constitutes a 'foreigner' is open to interpretation. Some consider the pre-First World War wing-half Alex Bell as such, because he was born in South Africa, but he belonged to a Scottish family who returned to live in Scotland. Work permits used to make it almost impossible for overseas players to play in England although a loophole was found by some who joined Scottish clubs (where the rules were less strict) and then moved south. One player to exploit this opportunity was the Danish player, Ben Arentoft, who joined the club in 1971 and was the first of the modern foreign players. He had been preceded five years earlier by the Australian goalkeeper John Roberts, who played three first-team games and then had a season with the reserves. In March 1988 the Argentinian, Ossie Ardiles, made a brief (and painful) entry into the club's end of season push for promotion.

It was not until January 1993 that circumstances and Britain's membership of the European Union, made it more viable to sign foreign players. At this point the club brought in their greatest ever foreign signing, Henning Berg from Norway, and Patrik Andersson of Sweden, who had a greater reputation but never settled with the club. Of all the countries the Rovers have recruited from, they have had their greatest successes in Norway. Henning Berg was one of the club's greatest players of all time, a competitive yet technically perfect defender, while Lars Bohinen, never totally at ease with his position at the club, was nevertheless a talented man of rare skill. Morten Gamst

Pedersen has served the club nobly, a sadly misjudged player with a work rate and appetite for the game that few have equalled, while Stig Inge Bjørnebye was an experienced and solid left-back, even towards the end of a good career. Tore Pedersen was a sound centre back, although troubled by injury and not at his peak, and Martin Andresen was a better holding player than he was given credit for.

Over their eastern border, the returns from Sweden have been poor. Patrik Andersson never appeared to have the stamina for the English game, although he had an illustrious career after he left the club. Martin Dahlin had been one of the best strikers in the game, but he had a chronic back condition and his glory days were behind him. Anders Andersson and Niklas Gudmundsson were internationals but never equipped for a Premier League season. Nils-Eric Johansson gained a Carling Cup winners' medal but was never entirely convincing. It has only been since 2011 that any Swedish player has made an impression with Martin Olsson, signed by the club as a youngster, blossoming as a real prospect.

The club has preferred to concentrate its resources on northern Europeans and have seldom ventured into Latin Europe. Italy has proved barren with the unforgettable 'Ciccio' Grabbi squandering his talent, Dino Baggio perhaps the most disappointing foreign signing ever and the experienced Dario Marcolin no more than average. The best of the bunch was the injury-prone veteran Lorenzo Amoruso, surely the only Rover to have ever brought out a cookbook.

Spain provided Jordi González and few would complain about Michel Salgado, a Real Madrid legend who settled into Ewood life and played with fire and pride and never once mentioned the drop in playing standards between the Bernabeu and Ewood Park. Another Spanish international, Javier De Pedro, had a brief and forgettable spell with the club but hopefully young Rubén Rochina may have a more memorable career.

Greece provided the enigmatic and ephemeral George Donis and France the multi-talented Sébastien Pérez, who never attuned to life in Lancashire. In recent years France has started to rival Norway as an area for talent with the towering Chris Samba, Gael Givet and Steven N'Zonzi becoming firm favourites (although Marc Keller, Youri Djorkaeff and Kaba Diawara stayed for only brief spells).

Stéphane Henchoz is unchallenged as the best Swiss player, having little opposition. Oumar Kondé was at the start of his career and Johann Vogel at the end of it, and neither stayed long. The best German was Markus Babbel, his only rivals being a one-appearance goalkeeper, Claus Reitmaier, and a young talent, Sergio Peter, who never really developed. Dutch players almost mirror the German effort with another utility defender, André Ooijer by far the most able, the other two – Richard Witschge and Maceo Rigters – making only negligible contributions.

Turkey provided the incomparable Tugay, although other seasoned internationals Hakan Şükür, Hakan Ünsal and Yildiray Baştürk all disappointed.

Only five players from the former Eastern bloc have played for the club – the Georgian Zurab Khizanishvili, Vratislav Gresko from Slovakia, Nikola Kalinić from Croatia, Radosav Petrović from Serbia and Simon Vukčević from Montenegro.

In the last few years African players have become more common. At one time there were three South Africans, Aaron Mokoena, Benni McCarthy and Elrio Van Heerden on the books. There was also, for half a season, two Dioufs from Senegal, the famous (or infamous) El Hadji and Mame Biram on loan from Manchester United. In 2011, Yakubu became the first Nigerian to wear the blue and white while Benjani came from Zimbabwe.

After it appeared that the brief loan spell of Ossie Ardiles was going to be the club's only taste of South America, there has actually been a rush of players – Franco Di Santo and Mauro Formica from Argentina, Carlos Villanueva from Chile, Paraguayan Roque Santa Cruz and the Brazilian Bruno Ribeiro.

The only players from Asia have been the Israeli Eyal Berkovic, and Florent Sinama-Pongolle from the Island of Réunion, whose birthplaces both come under the footballing control of UEFA. The only West Indian has been Dwight Yorke, from the tiny island of Tobago, although London-born Jason Roberts played international football for Grenada. From down under have come the Aussies Lucas Neill, Brett Emerton and Vince Grella and a rare bird, a Kiwi, in the inspiring form of Ryan Nelsen. Last but not least was the United States' example of goalkeeping perfection, Brad Friedel.

GOALKEEPING STATISTICS

Minutes per goal (total minutes played divided by the goals conceded):

Jim Arnold	140
John Filan	89
James Crabtree	83
Tim Flowers	80
Bobby Mimms	79
John Barton	78
Brad Friedel	75
Alan Kelly	74
Roger Jones	74
Terry Gennoe	74

Clean Sheet percentage:

Jim Arnold	57
James Crabtree	42
Alan Kelly	35
Bobby Mimms	34
Nat Walton	34
Paul Bradshaw	34
Brad Friedel	33
Tim Flowers	32

Penalty record:

Goalkeeper	Total faced	Conceded	Saved	Missed	Saved rebound scored	Woodwork rebound scored
Brad Friedel	40	28	11		1	
Terry Gennoe	38	26	10	2		
Jock Crawford	29	21	4	3	1	
Roger Jones	27	22	3	2		
Reg Elvy	24	17	4	1	2	
Billy McIver	22	12	4	4	1	1
Ronnie Sewell	21	14	4	3		
Harry Leyland	20	16	1	3		
Alf Robinson	19	13	3	3		
Fred Else	18	12	2	2	2	
Tim Flowers	18	13	3	2		
John Butcher	15	9	4	2		

Longest unbeaten run:

Goalkeeper	Mins
Adam Blacklaw	582
Jim Arnold	556
Tim Flowers	503
George Marks	454
Bobby Mimms	441
Roger Jones	440
John Barton	420
John Butcher	420
Fred Else	398

IF ON A WINTER'S DAY A TRAVELLER

Moscow in November was not a destination the Rovers' players had in mind when they celebrated their Premier League triumph on the pitch at Anfield in May 1995. Unfortunately the draw for the European Cup was not kind – Spartak Moscow, Legia Warszawa and Rosenborg in the group stage. Moscow was all they had been led to expect – snow, a frozen pitch, temperatures of -10°C and a dire journey. The balance of the team had been altered by the tinkering of the new manager, Ray Harford, who was attempting to step up from his coaching role. One of his fateful decisions was to smooth back David Batty, who had missed most of the previous season, by playing him out of position, wide on the left. It was not to the liking of the player and worst of all it required close co-operation with the left-back Graeme Le Saux. Ill feeling between the two had been gathering on the training ground, but no-one could have predicted the drama to come. The *Guardian* described it thus:

> The two [Batty and Le Saux] squared up to each other after just four minutes with the game still goalless. They clattered into one another as the ball rolled into touch, trading insults, moved on to pushing and shoving and then Le Saux appeared to throw a left hook into Batty's throat.

Needless to say the press had a field day, although the one to profit most was the Spartak coach, Oleg Romantsev, who not only gained an easy victory but was able to pass on a quote that made the pages of many a football anthology – 'Before the match I told my players that we will be playing against eleven guys ready to fight for each other for ninety minutes – not with each other.'

The club did its best to make the incident go away, although the hapless Harford displayed his inexperience of handling the press. UEFA suspended both players and with time the furore died. Both players have given their retrospective accounts of the fracas but elucidation remains obscure.

It was not the first time that Rovers' players had exchanged blows on the field. The whimsical Irishman, Eamonn Rogers, once landed a crisp right-hander in the face of his wing partner, Brian Hill, although standards at the club were so low that nobody bothered to comment.

MALE MODEL

If the intellectual *Guardian*-reading Le Saux was viewed with suspicion, it would be interesting to know what his team-mates would have made of Stig Inge Bjørnebye. A thoughtful, deeply intelligent man, he sought to understand the melancholia to which he became subject, by writing. A friend, Rebekka

Nøkling, introduced him to one of her own friends, the famous Norwegian artist, Tone Dietrichson. Nøkling's insight was odd as Aksel Kjaer Vidnes noted in her essay on their subsequent professional involvement 'The Art of Influencing (Each Other)', 'The unlikely collaboration had been important to both of them. They had to go searching for a common platform where there was seemingly none, the artist and the athlete.'

They found symbiosis in their art. Bjørnebye became Dietrichson's model and at Nøkling's suggestion 'Book by Stig, paintings by Tone,' presented an exhibition 'Mirror of Reflections' juxtaposing Bjørnebye's writing with Dietrichson's artwork.

DID YOU KNOW?

Members of the media repeatedly inform everyone that Jack Walker bought the title for Blackburn. In fact his net expenditure on transfers was just £20.5 million in the period from December 1990 to August 2000. In the period from November 2000 to February 2010 the Walker Trust had a net income on transfer dealings of £8.6 million.

All eleven members of the Rovers side that won the FA Youth Cup in 1959 subsequently played in the Football League although Paddy Mulvey's appearances for Accrington Stanley were subsequently annulled when the team failed to complete the season.

In the days when all clubs in the Football League kicked off the season at the same time, there was always considerable interest in the first goal scored. In 1968 the Rovers claimed the honour when Eamonn Rogers converted a first-minute penalty against Derby County. At the end of the campaign Malcolm Darling scored the last goal of the season.

THE FIRST ELEVEN

The most reproduced line-up in the club's history is probably the first, which took the field at Church on 11 December 1875. It was:

T. Greenwood, Baldwin, A. Birtwistle, Syckelmore, Thomas, Duckworth, H. Greenwood, Lewis, Dean, Constantine, R. Birtwistle.

Greenwood, Thomas
b. Blackburn 1856
d. Rossall Beach, Fleetwood 22 April 1911
The Greenwood family had taken the first step to affluence when William Greenwood kept the White Bull Hotel on Salford Bridge. His son, Richard, moved quickly to join the local entrepreneurs who were opening cotton mills and by 1881 the family had a mill employing 280 people. By then the third generation ran the business, namely the three youngest sons Thomas, Henry and Doc. The oldest, William, lived in Wellington Street, already having made enough money to retire, and the second, Richard, was at one time president of the Cotton Employers' Association. The three youngest sons all played for the Rovers, Thomas being the original goalkeeper and captain although he did not play long, having performed both functions with the Blackburn Ramblers from 1873. By 1901 he was already retired and living in Thornton.

Baldwin, John
b. Blackburn 1856
d. Blackburn 21 August 1918
John Baldwin's father came from Grindleton, where he had an iron foundry which employed 22 men and 8 boys. He married Mary Dean, a Blackburn woman ten years older than him, and for a time the family lived in Blackburn. John was born in Park View Crescent, three houses away from the Greenwood family. By 1881 his father had passed away and the family was in Grindleton, where John managed the iron foundry. They had substantial property in the village and by the turn of the century his mother, Mary, John and his sister, Ada, lived on the rents from their estate. Baldwin died at his home in Carlisle Street. He was the Rovers' first right-back although his career was brief.

Birtwistle, Alfred 'Fred'
b. Great Harwood 1850
d. Blackburn 10 February 1921
Fred Birtwistle played left-back in the club's first ever game but his appearances for the next three seasons lack documentation. By the time the Rovers entered the FA Cup for the first time he partnered Doc Haydock at full back but soon lost his place when Fergie Suter came from Darwen. Thereafter his only opportunities came when pressed into service as an emergency forward. He was a relative of the well-known Richard Birtwistle, his grandfather David being the brother of Richard's great grandfather Robert. The son of William Birtwistle of Lower Fold, Great Harwood, who was a cotton manufacturer, Fred became a farmer and cotton manufacturer at Yew Tree House, Great Harwood, but by the turn of the century was concentrating on the cotton rather than agriculture. He became a director of the family firm,

Birtwistle and Fielden. At the Southport Sports in 1882 he finished second in the 120 yards against many of the best sprinters in Lancashire. In the heats he ran 12.4 seconds for 112 yards. He also played cricket for Great Harwood and was good enough to play for the Lancashire County amateur team. A keen shooter and huntsman he was an avid follower of the Pendle Forest Hunt.

Syckelmore, Thomas Joseph

b. Tonbridge 1848

d. Blackburn 26 November 1929

The son of a man from Maidstone who had a small firm specialising in trademarks, Syckelmore was educated at Tonbridge School between 1861 and 1866. In 1865 he became a member of the football XIII. He moved on to St John's College, Cambridge, and gained his BA in 1870. He then came to Blackburn to teach classics and mathematics at the Queen Elizabeth Grammar School until he retired in 1894. He originally took lodgings in Preston Road but married Ann, a local girl, and took a house in Park Avenue. He remained in the town all his life, dying at his home in Alma Street in 1929. After playing in the first game at wing-half he appeared little although he once kept goal in an emergency. He was well known as a member of the Literary Society and a keen swimmer at Peter Johnson's baths.

Thomas, Arthur

b. Torquay 1855

d. St Anne's 6 August 1923

Thomas' father Franklin was an upholsterer and cabinet maker from Rochester who set up business in Oxford, Torquay and Camberley before deciding that Blackburn was the place to be. Two of his sons, Franklin and Arthur, went into the family firm, Franklin taking over as manager (he later became an alderman in the town and was mayor from 1905 to 1911). Arthur moved to the cotton mills and became manager of Harry Ward's Swallow Street Mills, before leaving to work as an insurance commission agent. He became increasingly prosperous moving from Adelaide Terrace to Lancaster Place. His sister, Helen, married Thomas Greenwood, who she met at the Lancashire Rifle Volunteers where both men were officers. Thomas eventually rose to the rank of major, retiring in 1892 after 22 years' service. A keen amateur thespian, he was in demand both at the LRV and St Peter's Church because of the excellence of his acting. He was actively involved with the East Lancashire Territorials and when the First World War commenced volunteered and joined the East Lancashire Regiment. He was sent to train troops in the south and eventually retired with the rank of Lieutenant Colonel. His personal prosperity increased when he became a shareholder and director in Brown & Deighton Ltd, a Preston oil company. By coincidence he died a month later than his brother, Harry Talbot Thomas, who had worked his way up with the Manchester and Liverpool District Bank. Both men retired to Lytham St Anne's and died there in the summer of 1923.

Duckworth, Walter Hindle

b. Blackburn 2 February 1857
d. Blackpool 1945

Walter's father, Henry, was a joiner and builder in Bridge Street who had such acumen for the trade that by 1870 he was employing 30 men and 5 boys. Walter was educated at Clitheroe Grammar School and became Rovers' first secretary. When he married in about 1880 he bought a house in Whalley Road but he was as adept a businessman as his father and started to open woodyards in nearby towns. He lived briefly in Blackpool but his largest woodyard was in Preston and he lived there most of his life, running the firm. He died in Blackpool just after his 88th birthday.

Lewis, John
b. Market Drayton 30 March 1855
d. Blackburn 13 January 1926
At the age of 20 Lewis and a Shrewsbury School alumnus, Arthur Constantine, came up with the original idea of forming the football team that became Blackburn Rovers. He became the first treasurer and an athletic, goalscoring forward who played for a few years as one of the twin centre men in a 2-2-6 formation. An injured ankle, suffered while ice skating, led to his retirement before the club won its first trophy, the Lancashire Cup. He had directed his energies to the embryonic administration of the game, helping form the Lancashire FA and forced to stop playing took up refereeing so that he became the foremost referee in the game. He refereed the FA Cup finals of 1895, 1897 and 1898 and after retiring in 1905 returned in 1920 to referee the final of the Olympic Games. He was a director of the Rovers until business commitments led to him resign in 1897. Four years later he became a member of the FA council and later its vice president. He had arrived in Blackburn when his father who was a Methodist lay preacher brought the family up from Shropshire. A committed charity worker, he gave his refereeing fees to good causes and was a luminary in the temperance movement, his sister forming the Teetotal Mission in Lees Street. He earned a good living as a carriage and motor body builder, working with his brother-in-law Thomas Lewis, and had a large house in Belgrave Road.

Dean, Thomas

b. Blackburn 9 March 1856
d. Blackburn 1920

Dean was the youngest of the seven children of John Dean who ran a slate and coal merchants business from 25 Richmond Terrace. Educated at Windermere School, Applethwaite, he had been playing with the Greenwood brothers at the Blackburn Ramblers, when only 17. He later followed his father in the slate and coal business and became managing director of Dean, Waddington & Co., the coal agents formed by Humphrey Waddington and Colonel Hargreaves. Subsequently he moved from his home in Feniscowles to Preston New Road and moved into cotton manufacture. He was an uncle of Lieutenant Percy Thompson Dean who won the Victoria Cross at Zeebrugge in April 1918 when the motor launch he commanded rescued the crews from the scuttled ships *Intrepid* and *Iphigenia* under heavy fire.

Constantine, Arthur

b. Blackburn 1 June 1857
d. West Ham 1923

Constantine was the person first contacted by John Lewis when he had the idea of forming a football club. He had been educated at Shrewsbury School and was therefore one of the few local men who had ever participated in organised sport. His father William was a toy dealer in King Street. Arthur became articled to a local solicitor and when he found himself left out of the team, started to play for Blackburn Law. He was still playing full-back for them in 1879 and was in goal for the Volunteer Firemen in 1883. The family moved to Tranmere, where William sold fancy goods and stationery and Arthur transferred his articles to a Merseyside solicitor.

Birtwistle, Richard

b. Haslingden 1853

d. Lytham St Anne's 16 December 1929

An original member of the Rovers he played in all the forward positions but was most often found on the right wing, employing the speed that brought him fame on the running track. In March 1880 he scored all five of the club's goals against Nottingham Forest. He started work as a bookkeeper at his father Micah's mill before becoming its manager. Later he became a yarn agent, working from his home on Whalley Old Road. He elected to stop playing and moved into football administration, attending the first meeting of the Lancashire FA and was a committee member for many years. He also served on the Rovers' committee, taking over as chairman until he relinquished the position in 1905. He served on the FA Council until 1927, when he was made a life member of the FA. His son H.H. Birtwistle succeeded him as a director of the Rovers.

FOR KING AND COUNTRY

Two world wars proved that death is an egalitarian force. Footballers were not exempt from military service and many returned heroes but some did not come home. In the First World War, Eddie Latheron, the club's international inside forward, lost his life at the Somme, seeking to bring to safety an injured colleague. In the Second World War, another inside forward, Albert Clarke, was killed on the beach at Normandy. Yet the club's war dead pre-dates even Latheron. Arthur Lea Birch, the son of the vicar of Blackburn, and a captain in the Queen's Own Royal West Kent Regiment, died of enteric fever when serving in the Egyptian campaign, at

Tani in the Sudan on 1 May 1885. Jimmy Love, the Scottish inside forward who was Lancashire's first professional when he joined Darwen and who once played for the Rovers when they were short of players, lost his life in the same campaign. He was killed at the siege of Alexandria in 1882. Albert Walsh, the son of the club's director J.W. Walsh, and who had played in the public practice game in 1916, was killed serving with the Royal Flying Corps in 1917. Also killed were two members of the Cotton family, the club's majority shareholders. James Shuttleworth, who played for the club in the Lancashire Senior Cup, lost his life in Flanders.

IF THE CAP FITS

The first man who has played for the Rovers to achieve the magic total of 100 caps was the Norwegian, Henning Berg. His total was overtaken by Turkey's Hakan Şükür, who retired with 112 international appearances to his name. The Republic of Ireland's Shay Given has moved well ahead and has 125 caps but is considering his international future. For a time he was running neck and neck with Aaron Mokoena, but after 107 caps the South African lost the captaincy of his country and his place in the national side. The only other player to have reached 100 caps is another Irishman, Damien Duff, who achieved his century at Euro 2012. Patrik Andersson of Sweden retired after 96 appearances, Tugay and Johann Vogel after 94. Brad Friedel could undoubtedly have surpassed the figure if he had not retired from international football after 81 appearances. Of players who still figure prominently with their countries, Brett Emerton with 92, Roque Santa Cruz (89), Zurab Khizanishvili (81), Lucas Neill

(83) and Morten Gamst Pedersen (73), have prospects of achieving the magic 100.

THE LANCASHIRE HOUSE

The Rovers had a Cambridge graduate (T.J. Syckelmore) in their first team and have had other Oxbridge men since then (Arthur Edge and Jack Lee). They had a man who became a barrister, William Waugh, in their second ever game, a solicitor in their early days (Jack Hargreaves) and have seen one of their Premiership-winning side (Stuart Ripley) go to university and then qualify as a solicitor. However, few would argue with the fact that R.W. Fairbrother stands supreme as the most erudite Rover of all time. Dr Fairbrother (TD, DSc, MD, FRCP, FCPath) was born on 28 April 1902 in Lancashire and graduated from Manchester University in 1923 with distinction in obstetrics. He worked on tropical diseases and virus research before becoming, in 1938, director of the clinical laboratory at Manchester Royal Infirmary. As well as all this, he served in the Army in the Second World War and was an accomplished sportsman having played for Blackburn Rovers when he was younger and was even capped for England in 1925/26. He was also a decent golfer and was a Cheshire County player.

THE PANTOMIME SEASON

From the start it should be understood that there were mitigating factors – it was March 1968 and the Ewood pitch was as wet as Ewood pitches often are in March. The club had already missed five penalties in the season (Ferguson, three, and Douglas and Sharples one each) so players were not exactly rushing to grab the ball when the referee, Mr James, pointed to the spot in the 52nd minute of the game against Crystal Palace. Mike Ferguson had created the chance with a perfect centre, which Malcolm Darling contrived to miss. Barrie Hole, following in, slammed the ball at goal and McCormick used his hands on the line to keep it out. John Coddington had to be admired for taking his captaincy duties seriously enough to decide that he would take the kick – he knew in doing so that he was facing John Jackson, a quality goalkeeper, and that he was hardly the most qualified spot-kicker in football. As he strode forward to grasp the ball, Coddington, a ruggedly built, red-headed centre-back, bristled with determination. There was no sign of hesitancy or nerves to cause doubts for the crowd. These arose, though, when he started walking back to the place where he started his run up – a spot mid-way between the halfway line and the edge of the penalty area. He turned, lowered his head and ran up. It appeared to take an age for him to reach the ball, but the crowning moment of the farce was still to come. His shot was weak, straight at the goalkeeper and positively rolled towards the goal. It was greeted with laughter rather than despair. Yet the best was still to come. The referee decided that Jackson had moved prematurely and ordered the kick to be retaken (there had to be a certain sympathy for the goalkeeper – seldom can a man have been required to stand motionless for such a time). Whether Coddington thought of handing his responsibilities to another player is not known. To be fair none of his team-mates expressed any visible desire to assume his role. Coddington carefully placed the ball on the spot and with the crowd incredulous, paced his run to the identical starting spot as before. Once again he started the long charge to the ball but not one spectator could have predicted what would happen next. Once he struck the ball it was obvious that his kicking technique had not changed in any respect. The ball rolled straight to Jackson, who had time to bend carefully down and gather it. This time the referee did not allow a reprieve. Thirteen minutes later he pointed to the spot again. This time Eamonn Rogers pre-empted debate by grabbing the ball. He placed it on the spot and with no signs of nerves, duly despatched it into the net.

DÉJÀ VU

'The trouble in this present season is that we have no sooner been lured into making up our minds on this or that point than something has happened to convince us that the conclusions were all wrong. The change in the offside rule has put most of our ideas "in the cart" as it were and we have been groping during the first four months for some way out.'

The words of Syd Puddefoot, written in January 1926.
Substitute 'manager' for 'offside rule' and the words could have applied to 2011

DÉJÀ VU (TWO)

'I am told that the season tickets sold amount to about one third of last year's sales and the empty look of patrons of the stands at the first home match of the season was calculated to give the directors pause (for thought).' *The Buff*, September 1914.

The response to the Rovers' Early Bird season ticket initiative in 2012 was that only about 2,000 tickets were taken up even though the prices were substantially discounted, and payment by instalments was possible. The club extended the deadline from the end of April to the start of August, during which period they recruited several new players to attract customers. Even so, the total season ticket sales only reached 8,000, a considerable drop from the previous year's 15,000. Only a couple of seasons earlier, when the club was under John Williams's guidance, the figure was in excess of 20,000.

The explanation for the 1914 decline was that war had been declared and many of the fans were unaware of where they would spend the following months. In fact by the turn of the year, 7,000 Blackburn men were in uniform. It is interesting to note that the combination of Venky's and Steve Kean wrought as much havoc on ticket sales as the Kaiser and the dreadnought German army.

FAMILY

Blackburn Rovers was a club built on the family; in their first ever team were the brothers Thomas and Harry Greenwood while their younger brother Doc joined them later, on his way to an international career with England. Also in the team were Richard and Alfred Birtwistle – Richard's great grandfather and Alfred's grandfather were brothers. Later Richard's brother Arthur played for the team. The Hargreaves brothers, Fred and Jack, sons of the Blackburn coroner, both became English internationals, Fred at wing-half, Jack at inside forward. In 1886 Rovers needed a goalkeeper for their game against Halliwell and asked the veteran Accrington goalkeeper, Dick Horne, to play. He belonged to a well-known sporting family from Huncoat but was reluctant to assist the Rovers because of their rivalry with Accrington. In deference to his family's feelings he agreed to play on condition it was under the pseudonym of Richards, a somewhat pointless disguise since he was immediately recognised by both fans and reporters. For a family with an aversion to the Rovers, their ideology proved reasonably flexible and two of his brothers, Dick and William, kept goal for them in the Football League. All of the three played cricket for Accrington as did another brother, Bobby, who was the most capable cricketer in the family. When growing up in Huncoat (their father became the Accrington coroner), the brothers would team-up with the boys of the Bankes family and take on the rest of the village.

Arthur Blackburn was born in Billington in 1877 but the family then moved to Mellor Brow, where his brother Fred was born a year later. The family later moved into the Windmill Inn in Mellor. Fred went on to play for England and there was a belief that Art might have joined him if he had not been out of the game with injury for some time. Historians have never identified Fred correctly because his christened name was John Thomas Alfred.

The brothers Stothert present a curious case that has caused a misunderstanding. The sons of Thomas Stothert, a chemist and druggist from Preston New Road, they were both noted sportsman at Leigh Grammar School. Bob, the elder, played rugby for a spell with Manchester Free Wanderers but in 1888 he was back in Blackburn playing football for Braeside. On 8 December 1888 he went down to watch the Rovers play Bolton in the new Football League.

Herbie Fecitt did not turn up and Rovers played with ten men until someone drew a Rovers' committee member's attention to the fact that Stothert was in the crowd. Despite his reluctance, he was induced to take the field and actually scored, but was only rewarded with jeers at his lack of skill. Three years later his brother Jimmy, a full-back, signed for the Rovers and this has led to the mistaken conclusion that it was he who played against Bolton. Although Stothert did play for the first team in friendly games, he never played in a competitive game and was so disillusioned that he used to guest illegally for local teams. Reported for playing for the Darwen Dimmocks he received a suspension from the FA, which became *sine die* when he was then spotted playing for Knuzden. This was later lifted and he played for Brierfield and then made it into the Football League with Lincoln City and Notts County. However, as a qualified chemist he had little scope for enhancing his football career.

A similar mistake has arisen in the case of James Hargreaves, who was brought up with his younger brother Josh, by their widowed mother in Harwood Street. Both were inside forwards and Josh became a regular in the Rovers team. James played in the Football League for Northwich and Ardwick but returned to Blackburn to play for the Rovers reserves. On the first day of the 1896 season, Josh was selected for Rovers but withdrew at the last moment, James taking his place. Perhaps understandably statisticians have missed this (James' one first-team appearance for the club) and he remains an unknown Rover. Around the same time the Garstang brothers, Jack and Harry joined the club. Jack played three first-team games but Harry was hit by injury and only played once, although he subsequently became a director of the club. He has been confused with Henry Garstang, who played full-back for the club a few years before. The cousins Jack Dewhurst and

Bill Bradshaw from Padiham played together as long-serving members of the Rovers, Bradshaw also playing for England. His brothers, Richard, John and Ernest were all on the Rovers books at one time or another and played for the reserve team. Meanwhile, the English internationals Kelly Houlker and Arthur Cowell were cousins.

During the First World War the club had high hopes of a full-back from Astley Bridge named James Birmingham. On one occasion he was unable to play (wartime withdrawals were common) but knowing how difficult it often was to obtain replacements, he sent along his brother Cyril, who played with him in Bolton junior football, as a centre forward. The Rovers appreciated the gesture, shuffled the side and allowed him to play, although he is another of those players whose appearance has gone unrecognised.

The first twins to sign for the clubs were local boys Thomas and Joseph Melling. Thomas was a regular goalscorer for the A, who signed in 1928, his brother signing two years later. The next were also local boys, Don and Peter Hargreaves, who signed in 1947. They were B team regulars until they were called up for National Service in the RAF in 1949. Don, a centre forward, was the best of the two (Peter was a left-back) and he played in a public practice game and signed part-time terms just before he left for the RAF. Two years stationed in Padstow did not allow either to progress their careers. In 1999 the Dunning twins, Richard and Darren, signed professional after being trainees with the club. It was initially thought that Richard was the better prospect but it was Darren who played for the first team. On 25 February 2012 the Olsson brothers became the first twins to play for the first team, a possibility created a month earlier when Marcus Olsson joined Martin at the club.

Not long after the end of the Second World War the greatest pair of brothers in the club's history was signed. The Clayton brothers, Ken and Ron, arrived courtesy of their local side, Preston North End, who were keen to sign the eldest, Ken, but were not as keen on his brother. Their father was not a man to be taken lightly and he sent the pair to Ewood, where they were taken on. Ronnie Clayton proved the better of the two, and subsequently captained England, but Ken was also a solid player. For a time they occupied the wing-half positions at the club. When Ken lost his first-team place to Mick McGrath, their father was considerably upset and as a consequence both submitted transfer requests. Fortunately the situation was resolved and Ronnie Clayton remained a one-club man. Soon after, the club had the local brothers, Brian and Barrie Ratcliffe on the books, although for a period they allowed them to join the Bolton Wanderers' youth set-up. Strangely the most promising appeared to be the stronger utility player, Brian, who played for the club in the Lancashire Senior Cup, but it was the more fragile but lightning fast Barrie who made it into the first team. Brian was certainly the better cricketer and became captain of East Lancashire.

There are a several examples of sons following illustrious fathers, although strangely none ever surpassed their achievements. The first was Bobby Murray, a goalkeeper from Brinscall and son of the Scottish international Johnny Murray, who was a foreman at the printworks in the village. Murray never settled into the first team, a curious reason being that he appeared to be ill-suited to the position, wanting to be perpetually involved and finding an outlet by prowling around his penalty area.

In between the wars the sons of the illustrious English internationals Jim Forrest and Bob Crompton, Jim Forrest junior and Wilf Crompton, played for the club but found living up to the legacy of a famous father a burden. Ernest Bracegirdle's son, Lance, was brought in for a pre-season public practice game but was not offered terms. In more recent times, Alex Jones and Andy Bell, the sons of the Rovers strikers George Jones and Norman Bell, have played in the reserve side but never graduated to the first team.

There is one occasion of a father and son playing in the same game. In April 1894 James Hunter made his debut in the Palatine League game against Liverpool. His father, the great Jack Hunter of Blackburn Olympic fame, was the Rovers trainer at the time and kept goal that day.

There are a couple of incidents of uncle and nephew playing for the team. Walter Crook was Derek Leaver's uncle and the great Bryan Douglas's nephew was Neil Wilkinson. Tony Bond, who played for the club in the Lancashire Senior Cup, was a nephew of the Rovers' international winger, Dickie Bond. Reports at the time of the arrival of David Bentley suggest that he was the grandson of Joseph Bentley, who played with the reserve team in 1953. Will Beesley, a member of the youth side that reached the final of the FA Youth Cup in 2012, is the grandson of Walter Joyce. John Byrom, the scoring sensation of the early 1960s was distantly related to Tommy Byrom, an inside forward whose career straddled the First World War and Ray Byrom, a reserve player just after the Second World War. Only one player who turned out for the Rovers in the FA Youth Cup has been the son of a player who did the same – Anthony Whealing followed his father of the same name. The early Scottish players, George Dewar and Tom Brandon, married the Duckworth sisters, Mary and Elizabeth, from Blackburn. At the start of the twentieth century, Bob Crompton and Sam McClure married the Ingham sisters, Ada and Bertha. When Mick Rathbone joined the Rovers he was introduced to his future wife, Julie, by her sister Lynn, who was at the time the girlfriend of John Bailey. The girls were the daughters of the old Rover, Roy Isherwood.

MASKELYNE UNMASKED

Dick Horne was not the first man to seek anonymity when he elected to play under a pseudonym. Within five years of the club being formed a player turned out for them under the name of S. Todd. The reason for the alias was that he played for their local rivals Witton, and he was the first attempt by the lordly Rovers to recruit a working-class local man. His name was Thomas Strachan but he was always known as 'Tot', so his alias is easy to work out.

In 1883 the Vale of Leven inside forward, Danny Friel, accepted an offer to play for Accrington. However, he was open to negotiation and before he played for the club joined the Rovers on a trip to Nottingham, where he appeared under the guise of 'Morris of Accrington'. The Rovers apparently failed to provide him with sufficient incentive because the following week he played for Accrington but soon went back home. A few months later at the start of a new season it became obvious what his requirements were as he joined Burnley on the strength of a job at Tillotsons. His appearance with the Rovers might have remained a secret if the club had not disclosed it to the *Sporting Chronicle* when they handed them their annual list of appearances. A similar disclosure on the same list was the name of the young Scottish player Andrew Hannah, who had played under the handle of 'F. Maskelyne', a name which appears strangely conspicuous for one anxious to remain unknown. More subtle was the recording of a player who turned out towards the end of the First World War as 'A. Newman', a name that aroused no suspicions and has only come to light because an examination of the records of the Football League show that his name was really D. Calder. Why the subterfuge was required is hard to explain although it may be that by playing he was somewhere he should not have been. If so *The Buff* helped by naming him as 'Mawman'.

Before the war the future great, Eddie Latheron, came down from the north-east for a trial with the reserves. He was such a great prospect that the need to keep his identity from other clubs was obvious, although calling him 'Trix' appeared too clever by half.

In more modern years the club has been less moved to inventiveness and simply used the common 'A.N. Other' or 'Trialist' to designate that they were not going to name the player concerned. Graeme Souness had cause to regret his lack of deviousness in the close season of 2004. In a pre-season friendly in Germany, he played a trialist whose name was not disclosed and who scored two goals. Unfortunately for Souness it had not dawned on the club that this is the age of information and a Rovers' fan had published the identity of the player on the internet within a day. It was disclosed that he was a 17-year-old Italian amateur named Rej Volpato, and he signed for Juventus a few days later.

Two men have managed to preserve their anonymity, a left-back who helped the club in a benefit game for the Sheffield Wednesday full-back, Hudson, in April 1889, and a centre forward who volunteered his services for the Ibrox Stadium Disaster Charity game against Celtic in 1902. The full-back at Sheffield Wednesday can be identified with reasonable certainty as Tom Brandon. Rovers informed the Sheffield club that they would play their first team except for this position, where Jim Southworth would not be playing. On the day several players pulled out and were replaced by reserves who were identified in the report. The fact that the club chose only to confirm the full back as 'A.N. Other' points towards him being on trial, and in August, Brandon joined the club. One A.N. Other that can be cleared up is the inside forward who played for the club at Middlesbrough in March 1888. Townley and Douglas were unable to travel because of last-minute hitches and the club had taken only one reserve player. Drafted in was Fred Robinson of Middlesbrough Waterloo, who the Lancashire reporters did not name but who was identified in papers in the north-east.

There are two strange cases of players who were not identified for years because the games in which they played were not adequately reported. Towards the end of the First World War, William Foolé, who had been a full-back with Astley Bridge, disclosed that he had kept goal for the Rovers in an end of season game at Halliwell, when the Rovers arrived without Woolfall and Fergie Suter had twisted his arm. Then, on the death of the international referee T.P. Campbell, it was revealed that he had played for the Rovers first team 57 years earlier. It was known that he had played with the reserves in 1889 but in March 1881, when aged 15, he was out riding with his aunt when the Rovers' wagonette, en route to Preston pulled up because they were a man short. They asked Campbell if he would play, he agreed and turned out in his riding breeches. Why his presence was required is hard to say, the Rovers beat the North End by sixteen goals. Hugh McIntyre decided to indulge their young recruit and teed up a goal, which made him the youngest scorer in the club's history. A similar case was that of Ernest Dodd. In October 1891 the club played a low-key friendly at Leek. They chose the opportunity to include a young Scot named McEwan, who was down for a trial. Unfortunately the train left early without the player on board. The local papers did not send reporters to cover the game so the event would have gone unremarked if the Beat reporter for the comprehensive *The Field* had not done his job and enquired from some players how the game went. He was informed of the player's non-arrival and that the team had not taken a reserve with them. Naturally enough he asked if they had found a deputy. The players told him that a man called Will Heath from Hanley had volunteered but they suspected that he might not be as good as he professed and instead, having met their old trainer Ted Murray, asked him to play. However, Murray was 41 and the players found a man called E. Dodd who looked the part. Asked how he fared they pointed out that the terrible conditions made football impossible but although it was hard to tell they believed he was a great prospect, even dubbing him 'the Welsh international'. They further added that if the Rovers wished to cultivate a female following they should undoubtedly sign him. The gullible reporter duly printed their words, unaware that the man in question was Ernest Dodd, a committee member who was in business in the town and who had been a centre forward in local football.

THE GREATEST ATHLETE

Duncan McKenzie is often cited as being the greatest athlete ever to play for Blackburn Rovers. The ability to jump over a standing Mini and throw a golf ball from one end of the field to the other are feats attributed to him. However, these were stunts, without a quantifiable result obtained in opposition against other men. In the early days of the club, players turned out regularly in local sports meetings. The Hornbys, Arthur and Harry, were noted sprinters and hurdlers. Dick Birtwistle and Joe Sowerbutts were others who gained success sprinting on the track but the best of the early men were the Southworth brothers, Jim and Jack. Jim held the edge – he won 20 races over 120 yards in two years and once came third in the Northern Counties 220 yards championship. Richard Porter was another flyer; in 1888 he won the 440 yards at the Rovers open sports day amid 'scenes of wild tumult.' He concentrated on his sprinting but found the handicap increasingly severe and his returns were consequently diminished. The pre-First World War centre-forward, Percy Dawson, was timed at 11 seconds for the 100 yards.

Before the First World War the club had an international class athlete, Benjamin Howard Baker, a reserve centre-half who wanted to be a goalkeeper. He was AAA high jump champion in 1910, 1912, 1913, 1919, 1920 and 1921 and Northern Counties champion in the high jump in 1911, 1912,1913, 1914, 1919, 1920 and 1921; 120 yards hurdles for 1921 and discus in 1920. He competed in the 1920 Olympics and on 5 June 1921 set a British high jump record of 6ft 5in. He also competed on occasions in the pole vault and hammer throw. That was a hard act to follow, but Percy Fish, the best athlete produced by Blackburn, did his best. A fine sprinter, he had the imposing physique that was to make him a shot putter with a national ranking. His finest performance came in 1921 when he finished third in both the shot and discus at the Northern Counties championship. This earned him the right to compete in both events at the AAA championships. The following season he was third again in the shot. He had moved from Blackburn Harriers to Salford Harriers and with his new club was part of the 4 x 440 yards relay team that in Dublin 1921 set an Irish All-comers record that stood for over ten years.

Preceding them had been J.J. Crook, who played football for Mill Hill Athletic but was much better known as a cross-country runner and steeplechaser. He was drafted in for the 1894 practice game when the club realised that they would not have enough players. His athletic career had blossomed after a slow start and in 1893 he had achieved the best result of his career when he finished third in the Northern Counties steeplechase, behind Fred Bacon who was to become the world record holder for a mile. A year earlier he had come third in the NCAA 440 yards hurdles, in his first attempt at the event. He was also a great cross-country runner and had been recruited by Salford Harriers to aid their nationally famous club in team events. However, he had shown signs of recognising that his career was on the wane and had been running for Nelson Harriers and Blackburn Harriers. He had once played for Blackburn Casuals and in 1889 joined Witton although his participation was negligible. During the First World War he was on the Rovers coaching staff and twice a week supervised junior players in the area, who were invited to train at Ewood at night so that the club might have players in the pipeline once the war ended. He was a very popular figure in this role and his unexpected death in 1917 was a severe blow to the club.

After the First World War it was uncommon to combine athletics and football but Marcus Bent ran the 100 metres for England when he was a schoolboy and John Curtis (the Blackpool one) was an English Schools hurdles champion. On a visit to Witton Park with the Rovers in 1992, Roy Wegerle jumped 7ft 0in, a height no athlete competing at Witton Park cleared until 1997. Ben Burgess jumped 6ft 4.75in when he was competing at school.

IT'S A MARATHON

The first ex-Rover to complete the London Marathon was the club's old goalkeeper, Terry Gennoe, in 1994. He was then

41 and the Rovers' educational officer. His time was 3 hours 40 minutes, in a painful run that raised £2,500 for Derrian House. In 2011 Dwight Yorke raised £10,575 for Vision, the charity he supports because of the fact that his son Harvey is visually impaired. He stepped in when Harvey's mother, Katie Price, could not run and completed the course in 3 hours, 31 minutes and 56 seconds. Less publicised was the run of Simon Barker in the Pony Marathon in Bolton in 1983. He was then an 18-year-old junior player and finished the course in 3 hours 40 minutes. As anyone who has ever ran the course which finishes up the infamous Plodder Lane will testify, Barker's run was undoubtedly the pick of the trio. From a fund raising point of view Yorke's was the most successful, although having rich friends helped with contributions of £1,000 each from Kenwyne Jones and Doug Ellis. Michael Gray completed the Great North Run (a half marathon) in 2010 in the time of 1 hour, 30 minutes and 8 seconds, and a year later in 1 hour, 36 minutes and 32 seconds, running to raise funds for the Sheffield Children's Hospital.

A NEIGHBOURLY AFFAIR, THE TOWN UP THE ROAD

'Good God – that one's mad.'
Mark Hughes' assessment of the Blackburn v Burnley derby

'People south of these towns don't understand how big this is. I get asked by silly reporters asking if it's like an All Blacks–Australia game. I've been to several All Blacks–Australia games and they are all yawn festivals compared to this thing.'
Ryan Nelsen

'I remember scoring two penalties against Burnley in 1983 and as I was running up to take the second, bricks were being thrown on the pitch. After scoring against Burnley in one game for Rovers I was leaving the ground and there was one of them outside in the car park waving a knife around. He asked me if I had seen Simon Garner because he wanted to stab him. I just said "no" and ran to the players' bar.'

Simon Garner

'That's what things were like. Darts welded together. There was a whisky bottle as well. I don't know how far back the rivalry goes and I don't know if it's more than just the closeness of the two towns but it's like gang warfare. It's been known for cars to be turned over and set on fire.'

Terry Gennoe

'I'd never seen anything like it. I saw one guy with a lump hammer breaking up the terraces. Then they got up on the roof and began tearing down the asbestos. It was absolutely scary: you thought someone was going to be killed. The police began a baton charge – although it would have been truncheons in those days – and it was absolute indiscriminate clubbing; young, old, everyone got it. The origins of the trouble were that we had lost, were going down and everyone at the Burnley end knew it.'

Alan Beecroft (Burnley fan) describing the dismantling of the Darwen End in 1983

'Nothing else has this feel. When Graeme Souness says it's something else, then you know it is, you'll not be exaggerating.'

Stan Ternent

'No-one who comes to this club from outside is aware how big this fixture is. When Graeme Souness was manager of Blackburn he said he was taken aback by this match.'

Graham Branch

'I've played in some cracking battles too, for Birmingham against Aston Villa, for Derby against Forest. I've seen fans slap goalies, had stones thrown at our team bus, been locked in a dressing room for two hours after the match while the danger subsided – yet this Lancashire derby is something else again. You would not believe the amount of animosity there is between these two neighbours, fuelled by their contrasting fortunes over the years.'

Robbie Savage

THE ONE-ARMED MAN

Throughout the world a handful of players have managed to play football at top class level, although they had only one arm. Charles Kettley, Arthur Lea and James Roberts (Wales), Hector Castro (Uruguay), Robert Schlienz (Germany), Jimmy Hasty (Ireland) and Hakan Söderstjerna (Sweden) overcame the lack of a limb to become outstanding players. During the First World War Blackburn Rovers selected a disabled man for one game. Bob Bibby had lost part of his arm during the hostilities. Before that he was a good sportsman who played right-half for Mount Pleasant and then Blackburn Trinity, the best amateur club in the town. He was more famous as a cricketer for his home village, Rishton, a middle-order batsman who made solid scores and was an athletic fielder. His father had died when he was young and his mother, Alice, worked in the cotton mills to support the family. The loss of his limb cost him his cricketing career but he continued to play football.

Rovers had not been enthusiastic about wartime football and sat out the first season. However, they realised they had made an error and faced with the prospect of losing out in the search for talent and conscious of the fact that their spectator numbers would dwindle, they re-entered the field. By then most of their squad were wearing military uniform and the club declined to bring in guest players and made up the numbers for the wartime league games with local youths or soldiers home on leave. Bob Bibby qualified on both counts and on 15 September 1917 he pulled on the famous blue and white halves. Unfortunately he was not fully recovered from his injuries, and was playing out of position on the right wing so he was not a great success, but he still made a first-team appearance for a famous top-flight club.

DID YOU KNOW?

Billy Davies once scored a memorable goal when he dribbled through the entire defence before slipping the ball home. No camera caught the action but an enterprising pioneer of the new movie industry decided to replicate the action. After taking accounts from all and sundry he asked the Rovers reserve players, suitably disguised in the appropriate shirts, to play the opposition. The cameras rolled and Davies worked his magic but as he was about to put the ball in the net, he trod on it and fell over. On tour in Hungary Davies made a similar sinuous dribble but as he rounded the goalkeeper he was felled by a punch that loosened several teeth. The goalkeeper did not even feign innocence but ran straight for the dressing room.

When John Lewis suggested forming the Rovers he had in mind a club for the sons of the town's wealthy citizens. The consequence was that later, working-class players became reluctant to play for the club even when invited. It was not until 1879 that a working-class player turned out for the club, the Scottish upholsterer, Hugh McIntyre. It paved the way for the first local mill worker, 'Tot' Strachan, a year later.

In their first season Rovers' income was £2 8s 0d (all from subscriptions). In the second season they were able to charge for admission and swelled their income to £8 12s 6d. In the first year they spent every penny. In the second they had two pence left over. In 2010/11 the club's income was £57.6 million of which £42.1 million came from the Premier League.

Only one Blackburn player has died from injuries received while playing for the club. Bob Marshall, a reserve full-back from Cheshire, was helped off Bloomfield Road on 27 December 1927 having received a blow to the stomach. He later appeared to have recovered and went to stay with a friend but during the night became ill and was taken to hospital. He died a week later from peritonitis.

WARTIME FOOTBALL

During the First World War the club never fielded the same team twice. When the regulars commenced to be called up, their places were often taken by men from junior football in the town. Many of the Rovers first team were stationed at Fulwood Barracks and at first they brought along players they had been stationed with. As time went on, this supply ceased. Many of the old players found it difficult to obtain leave to play for the club, although strangely one or two of them got permission to play for Preston North End, in away matches. Blackburn's problems in finding players became so bad that Preston North End volunteered them the pick of any players not chosen by them, but the Rovers only used the option on a couple of occasions. Just how bad things were in 1917 can be deduced by the fact that the RAMC, stationed in nearby Whalley, played a game against the Blackburn Recruiting Office. The following week three of the RAMC players, Fred Baughan, Sam Goodman and Albert Loveridge, were asked to play for the Rovers and Goodman (a fine cricketer in the leagues in Lancashire) went on to become something of a regular. Hearing of the Rovers' plight, South Liverpool wrote and offered the services of any players the Rovers might want. This led to Charles Welding and David Bottomore playing for the club. Borrowing players from other clubs was seldom an option because all clubs had problems but sometimes, as when the Rovers arrived at Stockport with nine men, local players stepped in. In this case James Bertenshaw was a Stockport reserve but Arthur Goddard of Altrincham St George's, just happened to be on the ground. Similarly finding themselves short at Stoke once, the hosts loaned Rovers two players, Eli Turner and Francis Underwood, the latter a goalkeeper.

William Young, a young centre-half had been spotted by Bolton Wanderers playing for Eccles and was asked to accompany the Wanderers on their visit to Ewood, as the twelfth man. He made the trip, found that the Rovers was the team who was a man short and started his involvement for the Wanderers by playing against them. Even a member of the training staff, Doc Crook, was drafted in for one game.

The identification of some wartime players can be taxing. An army gunner played both full-back positions, where he was said to 'use the touchline well and display good strength.' He was listed in reports as Froggitty and then Foggetty but army records indicate he was the son of an Irish career soldier, William Foggerty, who lived in Meols, Southport, for some time. To add to the confusion the son modified his surname. Alexander Patrick Fogerty enlisted in the RAMC in November 1904 but was discharged because he was 'not likely to become an efficient bugler'. He joined the Royal Navy but was released because he was 'unsuitable as an officer's servant'. Finally in December 1908 he enlisted with the Royal Regiment of Artillery. He should have made his debut two weeks earlier than he did, but he missed his train from Preston, where he was stationed, and despite just arriving in time, the Burnley gatemen would not believe that he was due to play and refused to admit him.

When football continued during the Second World War, the clubs were better prepared and guest players were much easier to obtain. There was also a realisation that even in adverse times it was necessary to find young players for the future. Of course there were still occasions when the team was left short-handed, never more so than at Stockport against Manchester United, on 28 December 1940. They arrived with seven players and found help hard to come by. The local reporter 'Busy Bee' had spotted a Stockport reserve, C. Wright, arrive and searched the ground for him but other footballers could not be located. Blackburn Rovers were not even well represented by officials and roped in the well known football men Harry Catterick and Ernest Barlow to conduct auditions on the terrace, among the twenty spectators who had volunteered. They found John Miller, who had a brother who played in the Football League, but for the last two places had to settle for two 16-year-olds, one of whom, Ken Hopwood was a goalkeeper. It was thought the other youngster, James Hallam, who was most exposed – 'He missed kicks, was knocked flat, derided with laughter, then cheered for his doggedness.' It later transpired that the *Northern Daily Telegraph* reporter, Harry Kay, had been offered a chance to play but decided that writing the news was a safer option that making it.

On several occasions servicemen came out of the crowd to fill gaps, one of them, Sergeant-Major William Bryson, scoring the winning goal against Burnley. The other side of the coin was that certain established players spent long spells guesting for the club and the Newcastle player, Tommy Pearson, became the darling of the wartime crowd for his class on the left wing.

MR FIX IT OR MR LOOSE TONGUE?

On Easter Monday 1903 the Rovers, who were relegation candidates, went to Goodison Park and against all the odds won 3–0. During the game the dissatisfaction of the fans grew and by the final whistle there were shouts that the game had been 'squared'. The story travelled across the Pennines to Grimsby, who were fellow relegation candidates. Within little time unsubstantiated stories became rife, including allegations that Bury had also colluded with the Rovers. Even so it was a shock when on 11 May the FA announced that a commission consisting of Messrs Sydney, Hart and McGregor, had been set up to examine the circumstances of the Everton game, following a complaint from Grimsby. A week later football was shocked by the verdict.

> We are of the opinion that Joseph Walmsley, the secretary of the Blackburn Rovers F.C. approached representatives of the Everton Club and endeavoured to arrange that the Rovers should be allowed to win the match. We are satisfied that so far as the Everton officials were concerned such efforts were not successful. We have not been able to obtain evidence to show whether or not similar offers were made to the players but the play shown on the occasion was such as to offer grounds for the gravest misgivings. In the absence of more evidence we give the players the benefit of the doubt and take no action. As regards Joseph Walmsley we are informed that he has been guilty of an offence involving the most serious consequences to the game in the estimation of the public and feel that he must be suspended from taking any further part in connection with the game. We are further of the opinion that the Everton directors neglected their duty in not reporting the matter to the F.A. and the Football League.

Walmsley was an unlikely candidate for the role of football villain. He had been a player with the Olympic and had worked his way up to become a manager of one of the Birtwistle mills, a position of some trust. Seven years before the incident he had taken over as secretary at the Rovers. Senior sources in the game, close to both Walmsley and the Everton directors, believed that Walmsley had made a jocular remark on the importance of the match, but it was not made with the intention of influencing the other side. Walmsley received significant support from some influential figures in the game, who believed that the findings of the commission were flawed and he was urged to appeal the decision. In August 1905 a Grimsby director, W.H. Bellamy, petitioned the FA for his suspension to be lifted. However, Walmsley had moved on in his life, had taken over the running of the Florence Inn and had no desire to return to football and so Bellamy withdrew the request.

SEVEN UP

Tommy Briggs came to Blackburn in November 1952. In his first part season he scored 9 goals, a fair return from 17 games. He followed this with 32 goals in a full season. By the time the Rovers played Bristol Rovers on 5 February 1955 he had already scored 23 goals. Yet you could sense that this was not going to be his day. The opposition had taken the lead when uncharacteristically Bill Eckersley got in a tangle, Bush centred and Roost scored with a rocket shot. It took until the 23rd minute before the Rovers equalised, courtesy of little Eddie Crossan, who steered home a header. A minute later Eckersley's embarrassment continued. In clearing an attack he slid over the touchline and wiped out a linesman. Ever the gentleman he helped the official to his feet and checked that he was alright, unaware that the game had continued, until Lumsden scored.

Briggs had been a menace as was his custom but his best efforts were thwarted, one by the post the other by a brilliant dive and flick of the hand by Radford, the Bristol goalkeeper. The reason that Briggs was a great goalscorer was simple – he never had another thought in his mind. The allegation was made that he had little skill, had not the footwork to beat an opponent and only moved in a straight line. However, that line was towards the goal, he was tough and virtually impossible to shake off the ball, and he could score with either foot or his head. In the 33rd minute, Briggs got his first reward. Crossan and Quigley supplied the artistry with an intricate passing movement, which ended when Quigley directed the ball to Briggs. His low drive was a goal from the moment it left his foot. Yet the Rovers still went in at half time a goal in arrears because Lambert scored Bristol's third.

The crucial moment came in the third minute of the second half. Mooney was chasing a lost cause as the ball appeared destined to pass out for a goal-kick, but an outrushing Radford brought him down on the edge of the penalty area, inches from the dead ball line. The award of an indirect free kick was contentious but from the angle it mattered little. Crossan sized up the position, floated it over Radford and Briggs arriving at the back post to bundled it over the line. The stalemate continued until the 62nd minute when Quigley flicked a pass to Langton on the halfway line. He had a step on the full-back and kept it all the way to the dead ball line when he pulled it back perfectly for Briggs. Now Briggs was up and running and his fourth goal was the finest of the afternoon. Bill Smith split the defence with a through pass and Briggs took it in his stride, beat four men by pace and then coolly placed his shot low, inside the post.

Briggs' fifth saw another side of the player. A scramble developed in the Bristol penalty area and while players hacked at the ball, Quigley had the shrewdest head. When he got the ball, he looked for Briggs, found him, and the centre forward got his shot away instantly.

Bristol were tiring and Briggs scored a sixth, hitting the ball on the volley from Mooney's fine centre. As the game reached its conclusion the Rovers were still going forward and in a late attack Langton went over in the penalty area. The referee pointed to the spot and Langton, who was the club's penalty-taker, grabbed the ball. It was the moment when Briggs displayed the modesty and team spirit that made him such an important club man. Despite the shouts of the crowd to give him the ball, he never evinced any interest in being allowed to take the kick. However, Langton was not going to deny him and strode over to hand him the ball. Briggs was seen to shake his head, some other players intervened to convince him that he should do so and after considerable hesitation, Briggs walked forward and drove his seventh goal into the net. There was one last reminder of the mannerisms of an age long gone. As he turned back to make his way back to the halfway line, his team-mates one by one, walked up to him and simply shook his hand.

Strangely, he scored another two goals in February but then hit a real scoring drought, getting just one goal in March and April and ending up with 33 for the season. He got 31 the next season and 32 after that but he lost his place to Peter Dobing and added only another three goals before bowing out, the greatest goalscorer the club had ever had. Speaking later of his seven goals, Briggs said:

You could say I was quietly pleased. Actually I should have scored 11 or 12. I hit the post a couple of times and missed one or two sitters. The match ball was presented to me and I sent it to the Bristol dressing room for them to sign. Their 'keeper refused but it didn't bother me. I didn't have his name on the ball but it certainly was covered with his fingerprints.

FOUR IN FIVE

Not even the great Tommy Briggs could match those five minutes on 16 September 1922 when Johnny McIntyre scored four goals. He was an unlikely candidate for the role of goalscorer, an inside forward whose striking of a ball was so wayward that the mill chimney behind the Darwen End was often referred to as McIntyre's chimney. Most of his career he had played at wing-half, but Sheffield Wednesday converted him to inside forward. In 1920/21 he scored 27 goals which prompted the Rovers to buy him. However, in 21 inside forward appearances for the Rovers he had scored just two goals.

In this match, he got his first goal in the 55th minute and then scored the next two at intervals of one minute. Perhaps fatigue set in, for his fourth took him a further two minutes. None of the goals was exceptional, but when analysed, his success was attributed to perfect positioning, although why he should suddenly have this purple patch in a Rovers career that brought 38 goals in 175 games is not explicable.

GARNER, GOAL HERO

Briggs' scoring record of 140 goals eventually fell to the cult hero, Simon Garner, who scored 168 goals, although in considerably more appearances than Briggs. Like Briggs, Garner had one game that surpassed the rest, on 10 September 1983 against Derby County. Unlike Briggs, he was up and running from the off. He scored his first in the 10th minute; Miller robbed Robertson on the halfway line and sped away. He hung over a perfect cross and Noel Brotherston met the ball perfectly, his thunderous header striking the crossbar. Garner reacted quickly and was first to the rebound, steering his header into the unguarded net. Two minutes later Miller lobbed a ball down the centre of the defence, the defenders dithered and Garner had all the invitation he needed to tuck the ball away. In the 22nd minute Lowey was felled on the edge of the area. Randell reacted quickly and flicked the free kick wide to Rathbone who crossed into the box. Garner was way too quick for the defence and his header completed his hat-trick.

Often players lose their desire after scoring so many goals. Derek Dougan once famously had four first-half goals against West Ham, and spent the second half looking like a man who has done his shift. Indeed, the game was being played out until 15 minutes from time Derby reduced the arrears. It was controversial, the player being several yards offside, a fact duly spotted by a furiously flagging linesman, who inexplicably was overruled by referee Seel. That probably worked in Garner's favour. Five minutes later he ghosted in and side-footed the ball in after a cross from the right had evaded everybody. Memories of Tommy Briggs were evoked three minutes from time. Futcher handled in the penalty area and the referee awarded the spot kick. At this point similarities disappeared – Garner was never going to have to be persuaded to take it. Totally confident he sent Cherry the wrong way, and placed it inside his right-hand post. His celebrations were certainly not muted.

IT'S STILL ABOUT A BALL

When **Sébastien Pérez** joined Blackburn Rovers in June 1998, he had been voted the best right-back in French football by the influential *France Football* magazine. Unhappily for him his career coincided with that of the great Lilian Thuram and he never received international recognition. He also suffered from a strange choice of clubs and his career drifted away without him ever capitalising on his fine talents. In 2007 he started to play beach football for ASPTT (Aix en Provence) and was drafted into the national team for the World Cup finals in Rio de Janeiro. Playing for a team coached by Eric Cantona and his brother Joel, he made his debut against Spain and scored two goals in his next game against Canada. At the end of the tournament he ended up with a third-place medal as France lost to Uruguay in the semi-finals but then beat Portugal in the third-place play-off.

Dario Marcolin made a record twenty-eight appearances for the Italian under-21 side but never received a full international cap. An honest if somewhat stereotyped midfield player, he had a loan spell with the Rovers before returning to play for Napoli, who then went bankrupt. In 2005 he started to play Futsal at the top level and at the age of 34 was called up for the international side. Around the same time, **Darren Dunning**, the stocky little midfield player from Scarborough who had left the club to join York City, was called up for the English Futsal squad for a tournament in France.

Edward Bateson was an all round sportsman at Giggleswick School where his best sport was athletics. He won several public schools' championships with his blistering pace, as well as important meetings at Powderhall and Grasmere. In 1922 he forced his way into the Skipton rugby team on the right wing and in January the following year won the first of six Yorkshire county caps. A year later Rovers invited him for a trial with the reserves and he was so successful that after just a week he made his debut. He retained his amateur status because he was required by Yorkshire for their championship campaign but a muscle strain received playing football cost him his rugby place. He therefore decided to sign professional with the Rovers but while he was recovering the club signed the gifted Joe Hulme and Bateson's opportunity had passed. Unable to return to rugby union he went professional with Wakefield Trinity and stayed there for five years, gaining a County Cup runners-up medal. A good cricketer with Settle, he played for East Lancashire and proved to be their finest ever boundary fielder.

A lively winger from Preston, **Ian Aitchison,** was a talented sportsman who was forced to decide whether to play football or rugby union. Despite appearing several times for the Rovers' reserves in three years with the club, he chose to make a career for himself in rugby. After playing as a junior for Preston Grasshoppers he joined Waterloo and played fly half between 1987 and 1995. He also represented Lancashire on several occasions. Subsequently he became coach and then director of rugby at Waterloo.

The famous **Albert Hornby** was an exceptional Blackburn sportsman who played the odd game for the Rovers. However, he preferred to play rugby in winter and cricket in summer. A long-serving member of Lancashire CC, he obtained seventeen centuries and played in three Test matches. He also played nine games for the England rugby team.

Arthur Paul was another long servant of Lancashire CC who was also an accomplished rugby player. He toured Australia and New Zealand in 1888 as a member of A.E. Stoddart's team.

Before he signed for Manchester United, **Kevin Moran** was a famous Gaelic footballer who won two All Ireland winners' medals.

Tom Booth was a centre-half before the First World War who went on to play for England. After the war he had considerable success at billiards and in 1927 made it to the first round of the English Amateur Championship, after winning the right by his success in the qualifying rounds.

A GAME UNIQUE TO BLACKBURN

A great buck match for £30 took place between James H. Ward of Blackburn and John Catlow of Wilpshire, in a field at Whitebirk on Saturday afternoon. Great interest was taken in the event which attracted between 500 and 600 persons. Both men are well-known players but they have never met before. The match, which was a single handed one, was played with 4 inch bucks and round headed sticks. Each player had 21 rises and during the progress of the match considerable betting was made. Ward was decidedly the favourite and 6 to 4 was freely laid on him. On the first rise Catlow took the lead but Ward immediately overtook him and finally won easily by 230 yards. The scoring was Ward 2,400 and Catlow 2,170 yards. The best hit made by each player was 140 yards.

Blackburn Standard, 10 April 1886

The game was played in Blackburn between 1850 and 1900 and was also known as 'tip cat' or 'guinea pig'. It was a dangerous game and countless locals were prosecuted for playing it in the streets. Basically the game consisted of hitting a buck with a 2ft-long stick. Jim Ward had won an English Cup winners' medal with Blackburn Olympic before he joined the Rovers. Although he became an English international, confusion has arisen in his identity and his second Christian name is usually given as Thomas, whereas it was actually Henry.

SOME YOU WIN:
THE ONES WHO GOT AWAY

In 1889 the Rovers secretary, Tom Mitchell, was despatched to Scotland with carte blanche to find the best goalkeeper money could buy. He headed straight to the home of the young Arbroath man, **Ned Doig**, and flashed his handful of sovereigns. However, he had to keep digging in his pocket – Doig had seen his team-mates defect south and knew the market. It was not until thirty gold pieces were sat on the table that Doig agreed to throw in his hand with the Rovers. The fee was unprecedented but Mitchell came home happy in the knowledge that he had signed a man known as 'a gem of a goalkeeper'.

Even a Scot can find Blackburn in November a grey, bleak and inhospitable place. Doig took up lodgings, played in the side that beat Notts County 9–1 and packed his bags the same night. Apparently he disliked the town. Possibly he was seriously concerned on the effect on his health of being so underworked in the Rovers goal.

Mitchell continued to frequent Scotland on his recruiting missions. One night in a local hostelry Mitchell received a tap on his shoulder and looking up found it was Doig. Mitchell informed the player that he was on his way to see him, for the return for a certain amount of sovereigns. Doig replied that he had regretted his actions and would like to return. Mitchell would have none of it, although he allowed Doig to keep four of the sovereigns as a gesture of good will. Soon after Doig joined Sunderland, the start of a long and illustrious career in the Football League, that also saw him play with Liverpool.

In the 1950s the Rovers had a scout in North Wales called Davies. He located two outstanding players, destined to become noted Welsh internationals, **Mike England** and his nephew, **Ron Davies**. The club trialled them and sent them back home, but happily somebody had a change of mind and asked Mike England back, at least ensuring they had the services of a centre-half who became one of the club's all time greats. However, they had reason to regret the loss of Davies, a centre forward who scored prolifically for Chester, Luton, Norwich, Southampton and Portsmouth.

Towards the end of 1996 the Rovers' Norwegian defender, Henning Berg, brought a youngster from the same Oslo suburb to Ewood for a trial. **John Carew**, even at 17, stood well over 6ft, had dreadlocks and plundered a hat trick in an A team game. In January 1997 he came for a reserve game against Leeds United, played havoc with the opposition but somehow missed getting on the score sheet. Rovers considered making him an offer but he was still at school and the club were reluctant to spend too much on an unknown. By the end of the year, however, it was too late. Vålerenga, who had just been relegated but received an injection of cash, tempted him to stay in Oslo. Carew became a world class player, a regular for Norway and ten years later entered the Premier League with Aston Villa.

In 1922 **Willis Edwards** had agreed to have a trial with the club but while the Rovers dilly-dallied, Chesterfield convinced him that the travel to Lancashire would be too much, paid £10 to his club and secured his services. An unusually mature, unspectacular player, it appeared for a time that the Rovers might have had reason for their doubts. However, once introduced to the first team he became an inspiration, a complete wing-half with skill at all aspects of the game. Leeds paid a huge fee and within a year he gained his first cap for England. He was rated by many as the finest wing-half of the inter-war years, an England captain on five occasions and the best passer of a ball in the game.

There was some excuse for the Rovers rejecting **Joe Mercer**, who was at the time 16 and a slowly developing wing-half playing in Cheshire. He played for the A team against Great Harwood. Subsequently he moved between several junior clubs before Everton signed him on amateur terms and under their tutelage they realised they had a kinetic player with leadership potential. By the start of the war he had gained five international caps and followed this with 22 wartime international appearances. He returned to the restarted Football League expecting to see out the remainder of his career in his native Merseyside but Arsenal had problems and saw Mercer as the man to lead them to safety. The assessment proved correct although few could have expected that he would prolong his career at such an exalted standard. In 1947/48 he captained the Gunners to the league title and two years later went up to receive the FA Cup in a season in which he was also Footballer of the Year. Two years later he was on the losing side at Wembley but the following season the Gunners were again league champions.

Some players got as far as the reserves but were still not rejected. **John Mahoney**, the son of a rugby league professional, made a handful of appearances for the Central League side at a time when he was playing for Ashton United. Commencing with the A team he was added to the reserve team squad at the start of September 1965 and made his debut against Sheffield United on 25 September. His start was propitious – he hit the crossbar with virtually his first touch – but by December he had trouble competing for a spot with a wealth of young talent which kept the club regularly high up in the Central League table. He sought a better opportunity and signed for Crewe, a platform that enabled him to be spotted by neighbouring Stoke. In the Potteries he found a long-term home, remaining for over ten years, a committed and passionate player with surprising quality in his passing. During this time he built a long international career and won the League Cup. After two seasons with Middlesbrough he joined his cousin, John Toshack, at Swansea but a broken leg terminated his career.

Another future international who played for the reserves but was not signed was **Jimmy Hampson**. In 1924 three players from Little Hulton (James Chadwick, Frank Grundy and Hampson) arrived on trial. Hampson made his reserve debut on 15 March 1924, playing inside forward, but despite further opportunities he was not offered terms. He had a trial with Manchester United, who also rejected him, neither noticing any signs of the voracious goalscorer he was to become. A year later Nelson placed him straight into the first team at centre forward and he commenced a career scoring goals at will. In his first season he scored hat-tricks in three consecutive games and attracted the attention of the large clubs. When they hesitated, Second Division Blackpool stepped in and his goalscoring feats increased. After scoring on his debut he scored 31 goals in 32 games and the following season was top scorer in the division with 40 goals. The season after that, his 45 goals in 41 games helped the club to the Second Division championship. Any thoughts that a step up would see him struggle were soon refuted when he scored 31 goals in his first season of top-class football, achieving in the process the record of the quickest 100 goals for one club – in 97 games. On 20 October 1930 he was selected for England against Northern Ireland and scored. He followed this up with two goals against Wales but was dropped for the Scotland game. The presence in English football of Dean, Camsell, Hodgson, Waring and Tilson, meant that it was not easy to hang on to the centre forward shirt and playing for a poor club did not help his cause. He was to play for

England again, in December 1932 against Austria, when he scored two goals but that was his last cap. His prolificacy was somewhat subdued by the lack of quality around him but he had seasonal tallies of 23 and 18 and had scored 21 in 25 games when tragedy struck. On board a yacht for an overnight fishing expedition, it collided with a Fleetwood trawler and he was thrown into the sea and drowned.

It was not the first time that the club had missed a future international centre forward from Bolton. After playing football at school, **Albert Shepherd** might have been lost to the game but he was spotted paying with his friends in the yard at Mitchell's boiler works. In the Bolton Sunday league with St Mark's he had scored 25 goals by the turn of the year and it was soon obvious that his forceful style and ability to score goals was worthy of higher-grade football. At the Temperance he continued his scoring exploits and was asked by the Rovers to play in their reserve side for the final games of the season. He was sufficiently impressive to be asked to return the following year but Bolton had been watching and stepped in and offered him 12s and 6d a week. When the player reported the following season the club had no space to include him and asked him to turn out for St Luke's, a side strong enough to feature in the Lancashire Junior Cup. Indeed it was in this competition that Shepherd confirmed his promise, scoring seven goals in a 10–1 win over Clitheroe, causing their goalkeeper, the old Rover Abe Knowles, to say, 'Shepherd gets the ball, shuts his eyes, the ball is in the net.' It was not long before a place was found for him in Bolton's first team and his scoring exploits there brought him caps for England. He scored 85 league goals in 115 appearances before being transferred to Newcastle. His scoring prolificacy continued but in 1911 he received an injury that kept him out for two years, and forced him to miss the FA Cup final. He had previously obtained both Championship and cup winners' medals with Newcastle, converting the first penalty ever scored in a FA Cup final, in 1910.

Ronnie Bolton, an apprentice mining engineer from Golborne, was spotted playing in the Lancashire Combination for Cromptons Recs in 1957. He was selected for a reserve game in October but was not offered terms. At the end of the season he signed for Bournemouth and became one of their all-time great players, an inside forward who could create and score goals.

Mickey Walsh, who became an international for the Republic of Ireland, was registered as an amateur with the Rovers in 1970 and 1971. Not rising beyond the A team, he joined his hometown club, Chorley, was spotted by Blackpool and not long later was top scorer in Division Two. He later became one of the few players to successfully play for a top European club, spending six seasons with Porto, during which he played in the UEFA Cup final.

Bringing in players for trials in the close season has become a feature of the modern game. Managers believe it gives them a better environment to view a potential recruit although it also creates a timeframe for a decision which can be detrimental. Among the players rejected have been **Róbert Vittek**, who went on to have a long career and score goals in the Slovakian national team, the Israeli international defenders **Tal Ben-Haim** and **Shimon Gershon**, and **Mounir El Hamdaoui**, who in 2009 was the Dutch footballer of the year. However, the most major misjudgement of all came in the summer of 2008, when the new manager, Paul Ince, was searching for a holding midfield player. **Anthony Annan**, a young player from Ghana who was playing in Norway, had a long trial and the chairman, John Williams, indicated that he had done well enough for a deal to be struck. However, Ince intervened, vetoed the transaction and instead spent more than twice the agreed figure to bring in the Australian, Vince Grella. Their subsequent careers could not be more of a contrast. In four seasons Grella completed 90 minutes on just sixteen occasions, his career completely side-tracked by a succession of niggling injuries. Annan has twice moved on, to Rosenborg and Schalke, and has been a much-valued commodity. In the World Cup of 2010, he earned great attention in the Ghana side, while Grella managed half a game with Australia.

SCORING GOALKEEPERS

Only two goalkeepers have scored for the club, and there was more than a century between these feats. The circumstances behind the goals could scarcely have been more different. When in 1881, Clitheroe provided inadequate opposition in the Lancashire Cup, the outfield players ran up eight goals and then declined to add to the tally. A ninth was scored with some reluctance but Howorth would countenance no such sympathy and dashed from his goal to score the tenth. Perhaps he realised that sporting life is ephemeral and that he would shortly be embarking on a life selling carbolic. He might also have been preserving his reputation for a report at the time stated, 'It rarely happens however that Howorth is out of form when his services are the most required. It is only when he has to encounter 3 or 4 shots in a match that he appears the most "dicky smithish" and no goalkeeper can shine under circumstances like those.'

It was on 21 February 2004 that Brad Friedel emulated Howorth. In the last minute of the game against Charlton, with the club a goal down, he went upfield for a corner. The ball was over hit but Gallagher returned it from the left and there was the green-shirted giant to fling his right foot and drive home the equaliser, although Andy Cole almost inadvertently blocked the shot. There was no happy ending. The club had been defensively deficient all season and in injury time they failed to contest a routine header, the ball dropped to Jensen and his drive restored the game to its former state, despite Friedel's groping fingertips.

In November 2011 Paul Robinson became the first top class goalkeeper to earn a penalty, when he came up for a corner in the last minute at Wigan and was kicked on the head as he headed the ball. The referee immediately awarded a penalty, which Yakubu converted to rescue a point.

WHO'S FOR TEA?

One of the tabloids once ran a spoof competition. They lined up four head shots, three of hirsute footballers, and one of the PG Tips monkey. The players were Bob Latchford, Trevor Hockey and Rovers' Eamonn Rogers – the aim of the competition was to identify the monkey.

LONG THROWS

Given Sam Allardyce's reputation, it was inevitable that when he managed the Rovers the club became labelled as a long-ball side. At the heart of the technique of getting the ball into the penalty area as quickly as possible, were the long throw-ins of Morten Gamst Pedersen – the sight of him towelling the ball on the touchline prior to launching the ball was an iconic image of the Allardyce years. As good an exponent of the art as the club has ever possessed, he once managed to throw the ball directly into the net.

Another throw-in expert who preceded Pedersen, was the Slovakian left-back, Vratislav Greško, who achieved similar distance without causing as much comment. Old wing-halves, from the days when clubs played 2-3-5 formations, actually considered it part of their duties – the right-half took throws on the right side, the left on the left side. Wing-halves with weak throws were tutored by the training staff, but did not relinquish their on-field duty.

In between the wars the best of the Rovers was Bill Imrie, recognised, alongside the great Sam Weaver, Bernard Robinson and Horace Burrows, as the best in the game. The *Blackburn Times* noted 'his prodigious throws were as useful as free kicks or corners and produced more than a few goals.' After the war Ronnie Clayton was supreme at the art. He even devoted a page of his autobiography *A Slave to Soccer* to an action sequence of photographs demonstrating the art of throwing in. Back in the early days of football the throw-in was taken one-handed. Conspicuous was the tiny full-back, Joe Beverley, a player who started with the Olympic, joined the Rovers, but later returned to the Olympic. When he played on the Olympic's narrow ground at Hole i' the Wall, he could hurl the ball the complete width of the field. Sometimes the ability to throw the ball into the penalty area was not deemed a necessity. Ian Miller, the right winger of the 1980s had a fine throw but Bobby Saxton never considered it a weapon worthy of exploitation. The ability to throw the ball long appears to depend on athleticism rather than size but even so those watching the academy side have been amazed by the ability of the tiny Raheem Hanley, to hurl the ball into the goalmouth.

FORMATIONS

A couple of Rovers players have played a major part in the development of football formations, although not when they were playing at the club. When football first started the unanimous formation was two backs, two half-backs and six forwards, split two to the right, two to the left and two up the centre. It took some ten years to change this, pulling a forward into the half-back line. In the pioneer years only one club attempted to field a different formation. Blackburn Olympic pre-empted the move to five forwards but used the spare man playing on his own in front of the goalkeeper, as the game's first sweeper. The duties normally fell to Joe Beverley, although he was sometimes moved into the forward line and was replaced by Squire Warburton, captain of the Olympic when they won the English Cup.

The 2-3-5 formation was enduring and it was not until about 1965 that it became obsolete and changes within the formation occurred. Originally the wing-halves directly opposed the wingers and the centre-half roamed the midfield, leaving the full-backs as the principal defenders. During the inter-war years, the centre-half moved back to a defensive role, the full-backs moved wide to face the wingers and the wing-halves moved into the midfield where they worked in combination with the inside forwards. When numbering was introduced the full-backs wore 2 and 3, the wing-halves 4 and 6, the inside forward 8 and 10, the wingers 7 and 11, the centre-half 5 and the centre forward 9. Players stuck to their allotted position and seldom interchanged. Until, that is, the early 1950s, when Manchester City produced the Revie plan. They had perfected it with their reserve side, using Johnny Williamson in the key role. An inside forward he was allocated the number 9 shirt but played deep in midfield. To compensate for the lack of a central forward, one of the inside forwards (8 and 10) would push up the middle. It was little more than a numbers shuffle but for a time wrought havoc on the English game. Its success depended on the centre-half (5) believing the opponent he was concentrating on stopping was the number 9. This resulted in him wandering out of position, leaving a gap which the inside forwards exploited. That it was successful was a comment on the absence of thinking about football tactics. Interestingly when the amateur side, the Northern Nomads, used the system in the final of the AFA Invitation Cup, they quickly secured a two-goal lead and repeatedly cut open their opposition. Then the opposition analysed the cause of their problems, stopped the centre-half wandering and pushed a wing-half up tight on the withdrawn centre forward. The opposition was Pegasus, the team comprised of Oxford and Cambridge graduates, who took twenty minutes to display a counter to the Revie plan that had fooled seasoned football men for over a year. Williamson came to the Rovers soon after, his role in the Revie plan having been well acknowledged, but he was disillusioned with the game and retired to become a grocer.

There was an amusing example of how the numbering of players was viewed with rigidity when in February 1966 West Ham came to Ewood Park for a FA Cup replay. Formations had commenced a rapid transformation. It was reasoned that goals would only come from getting more men forward and an inside forward was pushed up alongside the centre forward. It was countered by pulling back a wing-half to play alongside the centre-half, thus creating the 4-2-4 formation and all the clubs in the First Division, with the exception of Rovers were adapting to the change. Normally West Ham's half-back line, using the old convention, was Eddie Bovington, Ken Brown and Bobby Moore. In the new formation, Moore dropped deep alongside Brown and Bovington played the role of defensive midfield player. Before the game Ken Brown went down with tonsillitis and the decision was taken to drop Bovington back alongside Moore and bring in Ronnie Boyce in midfield, which in the parlance of the day amounted to two changes, one of them positional. However, the fact that Boyce was wearing Brown's number five shirt, and was playing in midfield, appeared to convince the reporters that West Ham had attempted to play some tactical formation never previously used. Coupled with the fact that Blackburn won 4–1 it was deemed to be an abysmal failure and Derek Hodgson in the *Daily Express* ran his article under the headline 'Egg Heads on Toast'. West Ham actually played the innovative 4-2-4, against the only team in the First Division clinging to the old 2-3-5 system. Despite the Rovers' dismal season that saw them relegated, they did not switch to 4-2-4 until the following year.

HARD MEN

No man in early football had the reputation for hardness that was attached to the Scottish upholsterer, **Hugh McIntyre**. There was an early demonstration of his capacity for the violent when he hit the Darwen goalkeeper, William Duxbury, so hard that he was rendered insensible. In these hard, pioneering days it was perhaps no surprise that Duxbury played on, when he was finally restored to consciousness. It appears that he accepted the assurance of his centre forward, Dr Gledhill, that he had suffered no damage though the competence of the good doctor was undermined by Duxbury's subsequent collapse. Removed to hospital, there were fears for his life, but he recovered and continued his career. During the First World War, several of the Turton players accused McIntyre of unnecessary violence although one of them, Alf Ottewill, claimed he tamed him. This appears to have been rose-tinted hindsight if the words of a fan of another village side, Withnell, are considered. Speaking after a Lancashire Cup tie against the Rovers he opined, 'If it wor nod for thad Mac wa could do somat but he freetens our lads.' Speaking around the turn of the century to the renowned Manchester journalist J.A.H. Catton, McIntyre lamented on a game gone soft, 'I do not know what football is coming to. If you sneeze nowadays behind a player, the referee blows his whistle.'

Sometimes the hard men are not the most obvious. The Blackburn side of the early 1950s was full of them. Some were immortalised by nickname, like **'Iron Man' Willie Kelly**, although sometimes nicknames mislead. **Jack Campbell** was nicknamed 'Nudger' which was not an understatement of a vigour that exceeded allowable levels but was a description of a series of tugs, trips and minor offences. The real hard men were not imposing men but **Eric Bell** and **Albert Nightingale**. When Nightingale left the club and the pair were opponents, the violence of their clashes became the stuff of legend in the town.

Equally deceptive was the pairing of **Glen Keeley** and **Derek Fazackerley**. Keeley, an excitable, and at times wild-tackling player had a reputation as a hard man but a striker who played against the pair had a different view. Whenever he played against the Rovers, he hoped that he would be marked by Keeley, who he contended was an easier opponent than Fazackerley. He preferred the odd wild tackle to any collision with Fazackerley, which shook a player to the core every time they made contact.

The crown of hardest man must be accorded to **John McNamee**. In November 1971, Rovers had experienced a culture shock when for the first time they experienced the physical demands of the Third Division. The defence was bullied and battered by juggernaut players and the confidence of fine players like goalkeeper Roger Jones and Fazackerley, was being undermined by the punishment they were suffering. At which point John McNamee swaggered into Ewood. McNamee had never been anything other than a hard man. The story goes that he was asked to leave his church team for his roughness – he was eight at the time. It has transpired that McNamee's attitude was his reaction to his lack of self esteem, brought upon him by the fact that he was born into a single-parent family and was brought up by an older sister. Within weeks he had transformed the Rovers' defence, rescued the careers of Jones and Fazackerley and created a platform on which the club could recover. There was never a doubt that he was a hard man, although his only dismissal for the Rovers was for dissent, somewhat analogous to Al Capone's conviction for tax evasion. Two outstanding memories of McNamee demonstrate the man. Bournemouth came north one evening with the highly rated and prolific striker Ted McDougall leading the attack. During one raid where he lost possession he was unwise enough to scythe down McNamee with a tackle that today would have produced a straight red card. The crowd hushed with anticipation but McNamee's reaction was surprising. Slowly clambering to his feet he fixed his eyes on McDougall, his face expressionless. The referee could not fail to be aware of the silent menace and intervened but knew that this was only the commencement. Not long afterwards Bournemouth obtained a corner and the referee, sure that the saga was unfolding, took the pair aside and lectured them. He then took up position where he could observe. The ball came across, was cleared and as the players moved upfield, McDougall was noticed flat on his back, motionless. The presumption was that McNamee had struck him and that is the view that Rovers' fans have retained. Yet it appears to be unlikely. The referee could have only took his eyes off the pair for a split second and McNamee would have had to possess the speed of Muhammad Ali to achieve that result. With hindsight it would appear that McDougall feigned the incident hoping to have McNamee sent off. What did happen was that McDougall had no influence on the rest of the game.

More conclusive was the action when the club played Port Vale and McNamee was exchanging knocks with a well-known hard, lower division striker, John Rudge. As the pair chased a through ball that eventually reached Roger Jones, Rudge claimed that he was being fouled by McNamee and started to appeal, while striking McNamee's back. The referee ignored him, play continued and Rudge fell full-length on the floor, where he lay, although he was not injured. Having seen the ball reach Jones, McNamee turned to head upfield, but found Rudge was prone in his path. Unwilling to go round him, he simply trampled over him, lengthways.

Although he might not have been classed as the hardest man, **Jock Hutton** was undoubtedly the strongest. He was known to demonstrate this by lifting team-mates using only his teeth.

GOAL-LINE CLEARANCES

Two types of action are remembered most in football – the scoring of a goal or a brilliant save. Overlooked is action that is just as crucial, the goal-line clearance. For some reason they slip from the memory. Forever remembered though will be the goal-line clearance made by Mick McGrath in the 1960 semi-final against Sheffield Wednesday. In the second half Derek Dougan had scored his second goal, and with a two-goal cushion, players and fans knew that their first Wembley final for 32 years was almost within their grasp. The premature elation almost brought disaster. From the kick-off Wednesday made a sudden and penetrative attack. The ball was played to Wilkinson and his angled shot was 2ft out of reach of Harry Leyland's groping left hand. Why Mick McGrath was on the goal line was a mystery but his position was perfect and he unceremoniously hoofed the ball to safety. He had been dubbed 'golden boot' following his late equalisers against Blackpool and Burnley, the latter completing an amazing recovery from three goals down. Eventually McGrath's golden touch deserted him and it was his own goal in the cup final that started the club on its way to defeat.

The greatest goal-line clearance ever made by a Blackburn player, unfortunately, had no impact on the result. At Tottenham in March 2010 the game was reaching its final stages and Rovers were already a beaten side. Paul Robinson had limped off and been replaced by Jason Brown, who had already gifted Tottenham a goal by allowing a shot to roll under his body. It was no surprise when he came out of his goal for a right wing cross and missed it. The ball fell to Pavlyuchenko, 8 yards out and with an unprotected goal to aim at. He lobbed the ball at the goal and turned to start celebrating but he had reckoned without the giant Chris

Samba. Facing his own goal he saw the ball drift over his head but somehow with immense athleticism, snaked a giant right leg upwards, his toe connected with the ball at a height some 6ft from the floor and turned the ball wide of the gaping net. The Tottenham manager, Harry Redknapp, stated afterwards that Samba was the one man in the world who could have made the clearance. It was a combination of great agility with split second timing and extraordinary spatial awareness.

THE RAFFLE

In 1886 the prize in the Rovers' raffle was a cottage, value £140. Tickets were on sale at 6d each but this was beyond the means of some fans, who formed syndicates to buy a ticket. Normally six men would put in one penny each and then would hold their own draw to decide who would be the holder of the ticket. Five Blackburn men agreed to do this but had difficulty in persuading the sixth, a gas meter inspector named Barker, to join in. Finally he reluctantly handed over his penny and then won the raffle to hold the ticket. On the day the club made the draw, he found that he had won the cottage, considerable riches for a working man. It would be nice to record that he lived there for years, but he died of smallpox in 1892.

THE WORST DECISION EVER

In 2007 Rovers faced West Ham at Ewood Park. Blackburn had serious hopes of finishing high enough to obtain a position in one of the European competitions while West

Ham were desperate to avoid relegation. Chris Samba's early strike had been cancelled by Carlos Tevez's penalty, a dubious award as the *Daily Mail* pointed out, 'Carlos Tevez went down under a sliding challenge from Brett Emerton in the 70th minute. Replays showed that little contact had been made and the Argentine was already slipping as he attempted to cut back inside his marker, but the officials decided it was a penalty.'

Minutes later West Ham played a corner across the 6-yard box, where Bowyer gained possession and fired at goal. Tugay cleared the ball off the line but the ball fell to Zamora who controlled the ball with his hand and drove the ball in. It struck Carlos Tevez, standing behind Brad Friedel on the goal line and bounced out but suddenly the referee's assistant, Jim Devine, was spotted flagging and after consultation Howard Webb awarded a goal. Subsequent replays of the incident showed that Zamora had handled, that the ball never reached let alone crossed the line and that in any case Tevez was offside and interfering with play. Mark Lawrenson asked on *Match of the Day*, 'How many reasons do you want for this not being a goal?'

The comments of the managers were:

Alan Curbishley, West Ham: 'Obviously the ball wasn't over the line but I'll take it.'

Mark Hughes, Blackburn: 'I am absolutely astounded by the decision. The only debate I felt was whether the ball was over the line. When I went to see the video the guy who cleared it was their man. He is clearly offside and interfering with play. Why the hell officials can't get that right I have no idea.'

Howard Webb said that his meeting with Mark Hughes after the game was 'amicable and constructive'. The only consequence of the match was that Devine was suspended from officiating in the Premier League for two weeks by the referees' commissioner Keith Hackett.

GOALKEEPERS ARE DIFFERENT

In the early days of football, goalkeepers were not the specialists that they are today. The role of goalkeeper was often handed to an outfield player and conversely many goalkeepers spent some of their careers playing out of goal. The great international goalkeeper Herbie Arthur, was originally a wing-half who found his speciality by accident. His contemporary goalkeepers at the club, Alf Woolfall and Roger Howorth were always prepared to play outfield if not selected in goal, Howorth being a good full-back and Woolfall a lively forward. Sam McClure joined the club in 1899 as a goalkeeper who had a reputation for being able to play anywhere. He was scheduled to make his debut in goal for the club but an injury to the centre-half resulted in him being switched to the half-back line. He remained at half-back for the rest of his career, although he did finally make one appearance in goal.

In 1892 Rovers' international inside forward, Nat Walton, was coming to the end of a long career. The club was having difficulty finding a goalkeeper and Walton volunteered to help out in a friendly against Ardwick. He played in the initial two reserve games and was then promoted to the first team and kept goal for the rest of the season.

Before the First World War, the international high jumper Benjamin Howard Baker was signed on amateur terms after playing centre-half for the Northern Nomads. He was a centre-half but expressed a wish to keep goal. He played for the Rovers in two reserve games but was then moved back to the half-back line. After the war he joined Liverpool and then Preston, endeavouring to become a goalkeeper, a position he had taken up with the Nomads. Neither club indulged him but eventually Everton gave him his chance. He moved on to Chelsea and gained two English international caps in goal.

Two men who kept goal for the club, Alan Fettis and Jimmy Crabtree, played in the forward line for Hull City and Rochdale, in emergencies, and scored goals.

DID YOU KNOW?

Daniel Burley Woolfall was president of FIFA from 1906 to 1918 and was the man who had the idea of starting a World Cup. He started his career in football administration as a committee man with the Rovers and served as secretary for a spell in the early years.

Mike Newell scored the fastest hat-trick in the history of the European Champions League when he scored his goals in nine minutes against Rosenborg. This record stood for sixteen years before being broken by Baftimbi Gomis of Lyon. Newell's three goals came from shots from both feet and a header.

The Italian defender Lorenzo Amoruso published a cookery book, *Love Food*. He also proposed to his fiancée on live television during the Italian version of the reality show *The Farm*.

Bob Crompton became the first footballer to own a motor car which he purchased in 1904. Few believed that a player could earn enough to have their own transport but Crompton was a highly successful plumber and he and his partner had patented a product that earned them the equivalent of five years' income for a professional footballer.

SHORT APPRENTICESHIPS

Reward is a random and often rare commodity – often footballers play for long periods without gaining any silverware. In almost eighteen years at the club that took in 674 first-team appearances, Derek Fazackerley won just one Third Division Championship medal. Two of the club's all-time great players, Ronnie Clayton and Bryan Douglas, had FA Cup runner-up medals to show for 665 and 503 appearances respectively. On the other hand in 1890, the goalkeeper Jack Horne, gained an FA Cup winners' medal in his fourth game for the club. In 2002 the feat was bettered by the Spanish striker, Yordi, who made his debut when he came on as a substitute in the Carling Cup final against Tottenham, and left the field with a winners' medal.

When Alan Shearer left the club in 1996, a year after helping win the Premiership title, one of his reasons for departing was that he wanted to continue winning medals and he thought that he had better chances elsewhere. Ten years later he retired, with just two FA Cup runners-up medals to show from his time at Newcastle. Of course Rovers fans don't take any satisfaction from this.

TRAVEL

In the early days travel was long and often uncomfortable. In 1900, the club's goalkeeper, Walter Whittaker, suffered travel sickness on the train journey to Derby. Despite being in considerable distress, he took the field, but was so ill that he remained in the dressing room at half time.

Trips to Northern Ireland were made on the ferry from Fleetwood to Belfast, across the notorious Irish Sea. On a particularly bad crossing the club captain, Johnny Forbes, heard considerable sounds of distress from the adjoining berth, which was shared by another Whittaker, Dick, and Nat Walton. Sympathetically he shouted, 'That's it Dicky, get it up. You'll be all the better for it Dicky.' A weak and groaning voice answered, 'Aw wish id wor Dicky.' It was Walton, who had been stricken by mal de mer.

RED CARDS

The change in interpretation of what constitutes a dismissal offence makes comparison between eras invalid as the following table demonstrates:

Era	Numbers of sendings off
1875 to 1915	7
1919 to 1939	7
1945 to 1965	5
1966 to 1980	17
1981 to 1990	16
1991 to 2000	41
2001 to April 2012	59

The club's first sending off was on 12 December 1891 and, almost predictably, their opponents were Burnley – Joe Lofthouse and Jack Stewart were sent off for fighting. Of the seven sendings off before the First World War, two were for Sam McClure whose 5th minute dismissal in 1903 was the earliest ever, until Garry Flitcroft was dismissed after 3 minutes of his debut in 1996. Between the wars, Tommy McLean was also sent off twice.

When coloured cards were introduced into the Football League in 1976, the first red card was shown to a Rovers player, Dave Wagstaffe who was dismissed for dissent. Lucas Neill has the most dismissals (six), followed by Craig Short and Tugay (five dismissals). Three players contrived to be dismissed even when not on the field. In 1973 Derek Fazackerley received a second warning for comments in the tunnel. Tim Flowers was sat on the bench at Coventry in 1998 when he was dismissed for comments to the referee. Gael Givet had been substituted when he was sent off for confronting the referee after the game at Fulham had ended in 2011.

Conversely Barry Ferguson received two yellow cards in 2004, but the referee neglected to send him off the field. Ryan Nelsen's integrity would never be questioned by any Rovers fan, which was fortunate for all concerned in February 2011. A native of Christchurch, New Zealand, he was shocked by the earthquake in the city and concerned for his family (his sister gave birth just half an hour after the quake which killed over 100 people). On the following Saturday, Nelsen wore a black armband as a personal demonstration but his afternoon ended when he was sent off in injury time. His subsequent suspension meant that he was not able to play the following week, and he was able to catch the first plane to Christchurch to see what he could do to help the victims.

WHO'S LAURIE CALLOWAY?

In the USA in the late 1990s an organisation named the World Sports Humanitarian Hall of Fame set up a selection committee to decide who had merited inclusion in its organisation. The members were Gerald Ford, the ex-president of the USA; Nadia Comaneci, Olympic gold medal-winning Romanian gymnast; Jackie Joyner-Kersee, Olympic gold medal-winning athlete and world record holder for the heptathlon; Jerry Kramer, legendary guard for the Green Bay Packers when they won the first two Superbowls; Floyd Patterson, once world heavyweight boxing champion; Stan Smith, a Wimbledon champion; Bill Steinkraus, Olympic gold medal-winning show jumper and Laurie Calloway. Calloway had been a reserve left-back with the Rovers who left to play in the NASL and remained in the country to coach. How he qualified with 'the great and the good' has not been explained, although he did play in an FA Youth Cup final.

WINNING BUT NO MEDAL

When Rovers won the Premiership in 1995, one of the reserve players was Richard Witschge, a Dutch international left winger who had come on loan just before the March transfer deadline and went back home at the end of the season. Back in Holland, in between derogatory comments on the style of play in the Premier League, he stated that he had been offered a Premiership winners' medal but had declined it so that Jason Wilcox would not miss out. Wilcox had been the regular left winger and had played 27 games before injury ended his season. Witschge played in one game (a loss) and would only have been able to receive a medal if special permission had been granted from the Premiership. The Rovers successfully applied for this permission for Jeff Kenna, who was one game short of the required number of appearances for an automatic medal and were prepared to do so for David Batty, but he declined, feeling he had not earned it. Recipients of Premiership medals were: Tim Flowers, Bobby Mimms, Henning Berg, Colin Hendry, Ian Pearce, Tony Gale, Graeme Le Saux, Jeff Kenna, Stuart Ripley, Tim Sherwood, Mark Atkins, Jason Wilcox, Alan Shearer, Chris Sutton, Mike Newell, Robbie Slater and Paul Warhurst.

TOP TRANSFERS

All the fees are approximates as some are undisclosed and some will vary depending on appearances, etc.

Highest transfer fee paid:

Andy Cole	£8,000,000	Manchester United
Barry Ferguson	£7,500,000	Rangers
Kevin Davies	£7,500,000	Southampton
Corrado Grabbi	£6,750,000	Ternana
Nikola Kalinić	£6,000,000	Hadjuk Split
Scott Dann	£5,700,000	Birmingham City
Christian Dailly	£5,350,000	Derby County
Craig Bellamy	£5,000,000	Newcastle United
Chris Sutton	£5,000,000	Norwich City
Ashley Ward	£4,500,000	Barnsley

Highest transfer fee received:

Phil Jones	£18,000,000	Manchester United
Roque Santa Cruz	£17,000,000	Manchester City
Damien Duff	£17,000,000	Chelsea
David Bentley	£15,000,000	Tottenham Hotspur
Alan Shearer	£15,000,000	Newcastle United
Chris Samba	£12,000,000	Anzhi Makhachkala
Chris Sutton	£10,000,000	Chelsea
Stephen Warnock	£8,000,000	Aston Villa
Craig Bellamy	£6,500,000	Liverpool
Nikola Kalinić	£6,000,000	Dnipro
David Dunn	£5,500,000	Birmingham City
Henning Berg	£5,000,000	Manchester United
Graeme Le Saux	£5,000,000	Chelsea

BIG SPENDERS

In the five years between Jack Walker's decision to finance Blackburn Rovers and winning the Premiership title in 1995, the club had a net transfer outlay of £25,835,000. By the time of his death five years later, this net expenditure had been reduced to £20,510,000. During the ten years the club was owned by the Walker Trust, transfer income exceeded transfer expenditure by £8,580,000. This meant that for twenty years, largely spent in the Premiership, the club's net transfer expenditure was £11,930,000, a figure that only emphasises the excellence of the management in this period. When Venky's took over the club they talked of investing £5m every transfer window. At the end of the third they had an excess of sales over purchases of £15.3m, thus making their investment £30.3m less than promised.

OTHER RIVALRIES

The natural catchment area for clubs in Lancashire is restricted by the sheer abundance of football teams playing in the League structure. Many people live in areas where they are within 10 miles of more than one club and the interaction of supporters in these areas is always lively and interesting. Such an area, between Blackburn and Preston incorporates Bamber Bridge and Higher Walton, where allegiances are divided. In 1948 a greengrocer from Bamber Bridge (a Preston fan), decided to recognise Rovers' relegation to the Second Division by filling a coffin with fruit and vegetables and ceremonially interring it. He promised Rovers fans he would exhume the coffin in the event of their promotion. From then on a tradition has arisen so that ceremonies of interment or exhumation are performed whenever either Blackburn Rovers or Preston North End are relegated or promoted. In 2011 with both clubs staring at relegation, the *Lancashire Post* ensured that the ritual would not be forgotten by running an article on it. Rovers escaped but Preston did not and in July a large crowd attended the procession on Station Road, Bamber Bridge. For local football fans it is essential to attend – followers of relegated clubs do so to emphasise their loyalty in hard times while the motives of the followers of the other club are less laudable, and the adjective that comes to mind is 'gloating'. Nevertheless it is a harmonious occasion, which has now become a means of raising money for charity and shows football rivalry in a better light. It is hard to imagine that a similar ceremony could be enacted in the hinterland between Blackburn and Burnley, without riot police and many casualties.

SCORING DEBUTS

11 December 1875	Richard Birtwistle
13 November 1880	Tom Jefferson
26 March 1881	Thomas Campbell
10 November 1883	Herbie Fecitt
27 September 1884	Arthur Birtwistle
19 January 1885	Tot Rostron
4 September 1886	William Whitehead
18 September 1886	Bill Townley
9 May 1887	Jack Southworth
8 December 1888	Bob Stothert
7 September 1889	Harry Campbell
27 September 1890	Jimmy Haydock
9 December 1893	Jack Sorley
15 September 1894	James Stuart
29 September 1894	J.J. Wade
26 December 1894	Willliam Walton
14 September 1895	Tim Tierney
23 November 1895	John Wilkie
20 February 1897	John Proudfoot
4 September 1897	George Hall
18 September 1897	Ben Hulse
2 September 1899	Albert Crook
14 October 1899	Arnold Whittaker
11 November 1899	James Law
17 October 1903	Albert Dunkley
17 February 1906	Joe Wilson
24 November 1906	Ernest Bracegirdle
25 January 1913	Danny Shea
20 March 1915	Tommy Byrom
30 August 1919	Ted Hawksworth
15 November 1919	William Fawcett

23 February 1920	Norman Rodgers
12 November 1921	Jock McKay
10 March 1923	Jack Crisp
25 August 1923	Ted Harper
7 February 1925	Sid Puddefoot
20 November 1926	Gil Shaw
28 April 1927	Bill Rankin
10 November 1928	Clarrie Bourton
31 August 1929	Cyril Gilhespy
14 September 1929	Wilf Crompton
4 January 1930	Arthur Cunliffe
29 August 1931	Ernie Thompson
10 March 1934	Thomas Brennan
17 November 1934	Jimmy Benson
12 October 1935	Felix McGrogan
16 January 1937	Jimmy Fraser
2 October 1937	Bob Mortimer
26 February 1938	Tommy Hargreaves
13 October 1945	Cecil Wyles
15 March 1947	Alex Venters
20 September 1947	Les Graham
18 November 1950	Derek Leaver
13 January 1951	Joe Harris
7 November 1951	Eddie Quigley
1 January 1952	Bill Holmes
8 March 1958	Tommy Johnston
7 March 1959	Jack Airey
20 April 1959	Andy McEvoy
1 September 1962	Alan Bradshaw
13 March 1964	George Jones
6 February 1965	Ben Anderson
13 November 1965	Malcolm Darling
20 August 1966	Alan Gilliver

14 August 1971	Gerry McDonald
17 August 1974	Ken Beamish
26 March 1977	Paul Round
26 December 1977	Keith Fear
25 February 1978	John Radford
27 August 1983	Chris Thompson
16 November 1991	Mike Newell
28 March 1992	Duncan Shearer
15 August 1992	Stuart Ripley
15 August 1992	Alan Shearer
3 April 1993	Kevin Gallacher
9 November 1993	Ian Pearce
14 October 1995	Lars Bohinen
30 January 1999	Matt Jansen
25 October 2000	Mark Hughes
16 August 2003	Brett Emerton
7 February 2004	Jon Stead
11 August 2007	Roque Santa Cruz
13 August 2011	Mauro Formica
17 September 2011	Yakubu

On 26 February 1938, Tommy Hargreaves, a local joiner, was selected to make his debut at Old Trafford. Soon after the kick-off Paddy Gallacher won the ball and found Len Butt. He slid a pass through the centre of the defence and Hargreaves coolly slipped clear of the defenders and stroked the ball home – he had scored after 1 minute of his debut. This feat has never been equalled. Scoring debuts are not rare but they do not average one per season. However the accolade for the most successful debut has to be awarded to a little right winger, Arnold Whittaker, who scored a first-half hat-trick, a feat that so enraged the Preston goalkeeper, Peter McBride, that he rushed after him and shook him by the throat.

DID YOU KNOW?

Over the years few players have done more to merit the antagonism of the Rovers' fans than the Manchester United goalkeeper, Harry Gregg. Having escaped scot free from knocking Bryan Douglas senseless with a swinging right hand and biting Barrie Ratcliffe, his luck finally ran out when he was spotted kicking Mike England.

In November 1971 the club almost descended to wartime levels of organisation. Shortly before the kick-off of the FA Cup tie against Port Vale, Barry Endean decided that he was not fit to play. The substitute, Tony Parkes, was promoted and no-one might have been any the wiser if there had been another player to act as substitute. A loud speaker appeal to Gerry McDonald, who was known to be in the crowd, to hurry to the dressing room, gave the game away.

During the days of Howard Kendall's management, economies were so necessary that letters could not be sent by first class post.

The facilities at the club's state-of-the-art training ground at Brockhall include accommodation for the trainee players and a canteen that specialises in the nutrition required by young footballers. Previously young players were placed in approved lodgings in town until in the early 1980s the club had the bright idea of buying one of the terraced houses on Nuttall Street and housing the best apprentices in it. The flaws were predictable. The players were unsupervised in the evenings. A daily cleaner came in but fought a losing battle and the players lived on chips they cooked themselves and pies from Leaver's shop on Bolton Road. One of the apprentices who survived these conditions was Franz Carr.

One of the greatest cricketers of all time, Sir Frank Worrell, once played cricket for the Rovers and scored 69 runs.

SOME WAITED LONGER

There is always urgency for a player brought into a team to score goals to grab his first, and most do so within at least a couple of months. However, some struggle as the following list demonstrates.

	Debut	First goal	Final Game (if never scored)	Time difference
Martin Britt	19/3/1966		26/10/1966	118 days*
Les Chappell	21/9/1968		23/4/1969	214 days
Kevin Davies	15/8/1998	5/12/1998		112 days
Barry Endean	30/10/1971	19/8/1972		197 days**
Francis Jeffers	23/8/2006	10/2/2007		171 days
Jason Roberts	19/8/2006	15/4/2007		142 days***
Robbie Fowler	24/9/2008		3/12/2008	70 days

* Adjusted for close season 103 days

** Adjusted for close season 96 days

*** Adjusted for time out with a broken metatarsal 97 days

Martin Britt was unable to play for a period of his spell at the club due to an arthritic knee problem, Francis Jeffers' first (and only) goal was a penalty, and there are other players with a statistically worse record than Fowler, although none had his reputation as a goalscorer.

LONG SERVICE

Including the First World War, Second World War and spells away from the club, here are the players with the longest time between their debut and final game for Blackburn Rovers.

Bob Crompton	22y 319d
Albert Houlker	21y 220d
Ronnie Clayton	18y 5d
Bobby Langton	17y 223d
Billy Bradshaw	16y 169d
Derek Fazackerley	15y 306d
Bob Pryde	15y 184d
John Byrom	15y 163d
Stuart Metcalfe	14y 347d
Walter Crook	14y 319d
Bryan Douglas	14y 213d
Harry Healless	14y 108d
David Dunn	13y 224d (to date)
Simon Garner	13y 204d
Jim Forrest	12y 169d
Bill Eckersley	12y 122d
Albert Walmsley	12y 111d
Fred Pickering	11y 333d
Johnny Orr	11y 223

Ted Harper	11y 126d
Colin Hendry	11y 57d
Jimmy Douglas	11y 51d
Eric Bell	11y 28d
Jack Patterson	10y 344d
Tom Brandon	10y 177d
Tony Parkes	10y 169d
Peter Holland	10y 127d
Eddie Latheron	10y 85d
Joe Hodkinson	10y 79d
Henning Berg	10y 78d
Jack Campbell	10y 51d

WHAT'S IN A NAME?

When names began to appear on the backs of shirts, complications were not envisaged and it was taken for granted that the player's surname would be displayed. The rule was first challenged by Jordi Cruyff at Manchester United, who was refused permission to use his forename. The rules had to be rethought because of the influx of foreign players, particularly those from countries like Turkey, where first names were commonly used. For instance Tugay's family name is Kerimoğlu but he has always been known as Tugay. Similarly players from Brazil and Portugal often adopt a football name which might be an amalgam of some of their names or an entirely original creation. As such there is a far less rigid attitude than previously with nicknames now permitted (although they have to be sanctioned by a special board set up by the Premier League). Morten Gamst Pedersen has always been known by his three names, the middle one being his mother's maiden name. After starting with the name Pedersen he decided to ask, and was granted, permission to use just his middle name on his shirt. A season later he changed it and by coincidence struck a spell of better form. A caller to Radio Rovers observed that he was glad to see Pedersen back as 'that Gamst was rubbish!' The Rovers have a unique record when it comes to dysorthographia in the kit room. In November 2007 at Old Trafford, David Bentley displayed 'Betnley' on his shirt and in March 2009 at Hull, Roque Santa Cruz sported 'Satna Cruz'. Coincidentally both players left the club at the end of the season.

THE KAMIKAZE HOOLIGAN

In the first week of January 1966, the Rovers team were just 9 minutes away from a home defeat, in front of 28,013 spectators, against bitter rivals Burnley. It was too much for Harry Heggie, a 19-year-old labourer from Monmouth Road in the town. He vaulted the perimeter wall, rushed at the Burnley goalkeeper, Adam Blacklaw, and struck him. It is inexplicable why the miscreant selected Blacklaw, 14 stones of glowering Scottish humanity, particularly when the assailant was not much more than half his size. Two factors allowed Heggie to escape from the consequences of his apparent death wish. Blacklaw was caught by surprise and before he could hand out retribution, other players, who were close at hand awaiting a corner, intervened to halt what would have been the most one-sided contest in sporting history. Within a week Heggie was in court and handed a £15 fine, the magistrate apparently taking pity on a man who clearly employed little logic in decision-making. Astonishingly three and a half years later the incident was repeated although the two youths who raced on and struck the Queens Park Rangers goalkeeper, Alan Spratley, did not make the mistake of having other players in the vicinity. They scaled the wall at the Blackburn end while play was at the other end and were therefore able to escape back into the crowd. However, one of them was detained by spectators and handed to the police. He was later sentenced to six months' youth detention.

THE CHANGING FACE OF ADVERTISEMENTS

In 1995 the Rovers goalkeeper Tim Flowers capitalised on his team winning the Premiership title to appear in an advertisement for Carling Black Label. The previous time that the club won a national title, the FA Cup of 1928, the goalkeeper Jock Crawford did the same, for Cephos.

NOW YOU SEE HIM

Geordie Anderson was just 21 when he came down from Edinburgh to play for Rovers in 1892. Although inexperienced he was a revelation, a wing-half of great power and speed and a shrewd prompter of the attack. The club were delighted with his play but off the field he was a constant problem for the committee. When he suddenly vacated his lodgings and disappeared from the town, with his team-mate Harry Marshall, they assumed (as he had planned) that they had fled back to Scotland. A week later the pair returned with expressions of innocence.

He later started training to be a professional sprinter, but his training regime clashed with his football training and the committee had to remind him of the terms of his contract. He responded by training so poorly that he received an official warning. He left the club for New Brighton and then started playing for Blackpool.

While in Blackburn he had married Hannah Ainsworth, the licensee of the Gardener's Arms on Great Bolton Street. She was nearly ten years his senior and had four children from her marriage to Joseph Ainsworth, a cab proprietor from Darwen. His death, two years after the birth of their only daughter, had forced her to become an independent woman, fully capable of supporting her family. When Anderson moved to Blackpool, she and the three youngest children went too, and she took over the running of a hotel in Oddfellow Street. Anderson tried to stay in the game when his playing days were over but obtained only a short-term contract in 1905 to prepare Cliftonville for their entry to the Irish League. Back in Blackpool the family moved to a boarding house in Victoria Street, which Anderson helped her run.

Anderson remained a popular figure in Blackpool, with regular contact with the football officials there. When in 1912 he found that an old colleague, William Almond, was experiencing ill health and financial hardship in Liverpool, he arranged a testimonial game between players from Blackpool and employees from the Windsor Ballroom. Then in the winter of 1920, with no prior warning, he simply disappeared. Officials from Blackpool FC aided his wife in the search for him but despite extensive inquiries he was never heard of again.

ON STRIKE

In the early pre-League days, the club often had difficulty in persuading their 'swells' to turn out in inclement weather. The situation grew so bad that their founder, John Lewis, left for a brief spell with Darwen because of the attitude of some of the players. Since football became better organised, and professional, there have been hardly any examples of players refusing to play. The outstanding one was that of Eamonn Rogers, in the 1960s, although he only refused to play right-back and had no objection to playing in a more natural position.

A young player, Peter Morris, once declined John Pickering's invitation to play left-back, although that was because he doubted his ability to cope with a first-team game in a position in which he did not feel at ease. However, since Venky's took over the club, Nikola Kalinić, El Hadji Diouf, Chris Samba and Gael Givet (twice) have all refused or been deemed not to be in the right mindset, to play for the club.

FREEMAN OF THE CITY OF LONDON

Recipients of this prestigious award include: Robert Baden-Powell, Winston Churchill, Benjamin Disraeli, Dwight D. Eisenhower, Bill Gates, Florence Nightingale, Theodore Roosevelt, Margaret Thatcher and . . . Aaron Mokoena. When the ex-Rover Mokoena received the award in 2010, he became only the second South African to be so honoured. The other man was Nelson Mandela.

MANAGERIAL RECORDS IN
THE PREMIERSHIP

The table shows the performances of each Blackburn manager
in the Premier League, since the competition's formation.

	P	W	D	L	F	A	Win %
Kenny Dalglish	126	72	28	26	211	121	57.1
Mark Hughes	147	58	39	50	181	176	39.5
Ray Harford	48	18	11	19	67	61	37.5
Sam Allardyce	76	26	22	28	86	108	34.2
Roy Hodgson	52	18	13	21	71	74	34.6
Graeme Souness	118	40	32	46	162	161	33.9
Tony Parkes	30	9	11	10	36	34	30.0
Brian Kidd	23	5	11	7	24	28	21.7
Steve Kean	59	13	13	33	72	110	22.0
Paul Ince	17	3	4	10	17	34	17.6

CLUB COLOURS

In their first ever game the Rovers turned out in black and
white stripes but by the time they took to the field again had
adopted the iconic blue and white halves that have remained
ever since. They were based on the design of the Malvern
College shirt, recommended by the Greenwood brothers who
had been educated there, but the green was changed to blue.
In addition they wore a white skull cap, embroidered with a
Maltese cross. The blue has been of varying shades and the
white and blue halves have changed position until after the
Second World War when they became fixed with the frontal
blue on the left-hand side. The back of the shirt was always

a reverse of the front until 2011. In one season the halves became quarters. Shirt sponsorship commenced in 1984 and has been as follows:

1984–91	ICI Perspex
1991–96	McEwan's Lager
1996–2000	CIS
2000–2	Time Computers
2002–3	AMD Processors
2003–5	HSA
2005–6	Lonsdale
2006–8	bet 24
2008–11	Crown Paints
2011–12	No sponsor was found so the emblem of the Prince's Trust was displayed.

DID YOU KNOW?

An old Rovers player, Peter Devine, has become a YouTube hit with the 'worst penalty of all time'. In 1991 playing for Lancaster City in a penalty shoot-out against Whitley Bay he was struck by cramp as he was about to hit the ball with his right foot. Off balance he dragged the ball against his other foot, from where it rolled about three yards.

In August 1901 the club signed a Manxman, David Boreland, who played a few reserve games. He later received a medal from the Royal Humane Society for saving a woman from drowning in the sea.

When Ally MacLeod led Scotland to World Cup failure in Argentina, Billy Connolly joked that 'MacLeod thinks tactics are a new kind of mint.'

There is a convention that no-one is sent off in pre-season friendly games. This unwritten rule was ignored in 1963 when the referee dismissed the Rovers' chairman, Jim Wilkinson, who had gone onto the field to make his views known to a Preston player.

AND THEN THERE WAS ONE

The Steve Kean revolution at the club ended one relatively recent but revered institution at Ewood Park – the walk round after the final game of the season. It was an opportunity the manager and his players used to pay tribute to those who had supported them through the season. The players had helped it flourish, at what has always been a family-based club, by bringing their youngsters to walk, toddle or be carried round. Even when relegated in 1999, Brian Kidd accompanied some decidedly shame-faced players on the lap. In 2011 the players made a half-hearted and somewhat truncated lap with no sign of a manager. In 2012 Paul Robinson walked around in the pouring rain, on his own.

CHAMPIONS

Here is the final Premier League table from 1994/95, the
season Blackburn Rovers were champions.

	Pld	W	D	L	F	A	Pts
Blackburn Rovers	**42**	**27**	**8**	**7**	**80**	**39**	**89**
Manchester United	42	26	10	6	77	28	88
Nottingham Forest	42	22	11	9	72	43	77
Liverpool	42	21	11	10	65	37	74
Leeds United	42	20	13	9	59	38	73
Newcastle United	42	20	12	10	67	47	72
Tottenham Hotspur	42	16	14	12	66	58	62
Queens Park Rangers	42	17	9	16	61	59	60
Wimbledon	42	15	11	16	48	65	56
Southampton	42	12	18	12	61	63	54
Chelsea	42	13	15	14	50	55	54
Arsenal	42	13	12	17	52	59	51
Sheffield Wednesday	42	13	12	17	49	57	51
West Ham United	42	13	11	18	44	48	50
Everton	42	11	17	14	44	51	50
Coventry City	42	12	14	16	44	62	50
Manchester City	42	12	13	17	53	64	49
Aston Villa	42	11	15	16	51	56	48
Crystal Palace	42	11	12	19	34	49	45
Norwich City	42	10	13	19	37	54	43
Leicester City	42	6	11	25	45	80	29
Ipswich Town	42	7	6	29	36	93	27

HOW THE PREMIERSHIP-WINNING SIDE OF 1995 WAS BUILT

Tim Flowers was signed from Southampton in November 1993 for a fee of £2.4 million which at the time was a world record for a goalkeeper.

Henning Berg was signed from Lillestrøm for £400,000 in January 1993.

Colin Hendry was signed from Manchester City for £700,000 in November 1991. This was the same sum as they had received from City when they sold him two years earlier. He had originally cost £30,000 from Dundee in March 1987.

Ian Pearce cost £300,000 from Chelsea in October 1993.

Graeme Le Saux was exchanged for Steve Livingstone in March 1993. Livingstone had originally cost £450,000.

Stuart Ripley cost £1.3 million from Southampton in July 1992.

Mark Atkins cost £45,000 when he was signed from Scunthorpe in March 1988.

Tim Sherwood cost £500,000 when he was signed from Norwich in March 1992.

Jason Wilcox came through the junior ranks at the club.

Alan Shearer was signed from Southampton for £3.3 million in June 1992.

Chris Sutton was signed from Norwich for £5 million in July 1994. This was a record fee for a transfer involving two British clubs.

Bobby Mimms came from Tottenham in December 1990 for a sum of £200,000.

Tony Gale signed on a free transfer in August 1994.

Jeff Kenna came during the season, costing £1.5 million from Southampton in March 1995.

Robbie Slater came from Lens in August 1994 for a fee of £300,000.

Mike Newell cost £1.1 million when he signed from Everton in August 1991.

Paul Warhurst cost £2.75 million from Sheffield Wednesday in August 1993.

The total expenditure on the team was £20.25 million. The players were subsequently sold for a combined figure of £50.4 million.

BLACKBURN ROVERS,
ALMOST CHAMPIONS OF THE WORLD

In 1885 public pressure was exerted to pit the English Cup winners, Blackburn Rovers, against the Scottish Cup winners, Queen's Park, for the unofficial championship of the world.

At the time the Scottish FA was incensed because of the vast number of Scots flocking to Lancashire to play professionally and therefore the game was only allowed to take place if the Rovers fielded an all-amateur side. The club could have turned the game down, but they had a fixture against the Olympic arranged for that day and therefore it made economic sense to send a side. Only five of the cup-winning side were eligible and the side was completed by two retired players, two men from Southport, one from Northwich and the old Olympian, Jack Hunter, who ironically was reclassified as an amateur after being forced to leave Sheffield because of professionalism. The side lost 7–1 but the gate receipts were good.

OBFUSCATION

A long-standing precedent exists for the obfuscation employed by Steve Kean. In December 1884 the club captain, Hugh McIntyre, was asked to explain an 8–1 defeat at the hands of the Corinthians. He advised the reporters the answer could be found in the Bible if they looked up the Eleventh Epistle to the Corinthians, chapter eight, first verse. Reporters were hoodwinked into believing that 'Mac' was being amazingly erudite until they discovered there is no Eleventh Epistle.

UNUSUAL CHRISTIAN NAMES

Genealogists will confirm that the range of Christian names up to the middle of the twentieth century were remarkably narrow. Anyone with the initial 'G' would almost certainly be George; 'R' would be Robert, with Ronald taking care of most of the rest; 'A' would be Albert or Arthur (very seldom Alan) and 'T' would be Thomas. The Rovers have had some early players with names that were amusing deviations from the norm. Of the players who made the first team, Dilworth Hartley was perhaps the strangest name. He was born in Bowland but brought up locally. Reserve players of the same era were Hardwell Bland, who left for America in search of work and Stonewall Howarth. Howarth's father came from Withnell, where stone walls are not uncommon, but probably took his name from the American general 'Stonewall' Jackson. Hardwell presumably arose from a family surname. Of a later generation was Tweedale Rigg from Rochdale, whose unusual name came from the surname of a connected family.

NONDA'S TALE

Of all the inspirational football stories of the ability to overcome handicaps, Shabani Nonda's story stands out. He was born in Bujumbura in Burundi, the ninth child of parents born in Zaire, who had come to work in the country. When the country gained its independence it promoted a long-lasting and bloody tribal war between the Hutu and Tutsi tribes. The savagery was extreme, even for the troubled continent and like most in the country, the Nondas grew accustomed when rising in the morning, to the sight of bodies strewn around. When Shabani was 16, the family joined the exodus over the border to the refugee camps in Tanzania. In the chaos, Shabani and a brother were separated from their family and became self-dependant. Conditions were harsh but it was the greatest normality that Shabani had known for some time and he resumed playing football. Improbably his potential was noted and he was recommended to one of the country's top clubs, Young Africans.

East Africa has produced great runners but not footballers and it was not an area of the world propitious for the launching of a world-class career. Nonda achieved as much as he could, blossoming into a fine, goalscoring forward, and is still the best player produced by the country. At this point the advantages of international competitions were demonstrated. His club Yanga became champions and played in the African Club Championship where they were drawn against South African opposition. Nonda was noticed and signed up by Vaal Professionals in Johannesburg to start his professional career.

South Africa came under the scrutiny of the football world to a far greater extent and at a time when he was considering an offer to play for Etoile of Kinshasa (he had decided to represent his parents' country, the Democratic Republic of the Congo) he was approached by the FIFA-registered football agent, Marcelo Houseman. Houseman persuaded Nonda to take the gamble of moving to Europe, with FC Zurich. It was, after the decision to flee to Tanzania, the defining moment of Nonda's life. Europe represented financial security but there were still plenty of opportunities for life to sour. A young African, on his own in a major European city finds many opportunities to indulge in excesses that impact on his career. Although he was fortunate to have contracted a reputable agent and had joined a caring club, he was isolated in Switzerland and lacked the expatriate support that he would have found in France.

Nonda concentrated on his football, however, and became top goalscorer in the country with 24 goals, a feat that coupled with the quality of his dynamic, driving play ensured that he would soon move on. Germany appeared the likely destination but Nonda was maturing and knew that culturally he would be more at home in France. He moved to Rennes, was a huge success and two years later moved to Monaco, in exchange for a French record fee of €19,800,000. At the pinnacle of his career, he scored a hat-trick against Real Madrid, before he experienced hard times again. In August 2003 he injured a cruciate knee ligament and surgery was required. The injury was extreme, even in a sport where they are not uncommon. It was April before he was able to play again but being able to take the field is not synonymous with returning to his previous state of fitness. While the repair of such injuries impacts little on the average man, a top class sportsman can seldom get back to the physical shape he was in. The successful learn to compromise, changing their style to fit in with the limitations imposed. For Nonda medical concerns were not over. He sustained a bad thigh injury, which sidelined him for a long period. With his contract expired he joined AS Roma but in December 2005, the knee was damaged again and he required further surgery. Although the explosive nature had gone from his play, he settled for being a hard, grafting player who never disappointed for effort and enthusiasm. He wound down his career at Blackburn and Galatasaray, finishing playing when released by the latter, who had more foreign players than was permitted under Turkish FA rules. His club had to decide who to release – Harry Kewell or him – and settled to keep the Australian. He contemplated a move to Greece but decided to move on without football.

He formed the Shabani Nonda Foundation, a charity originally designed to occupy the youth of the city of Kinshasa, who might otherwise have been idle and in trouble.

An annual football tournament was organised but it was soon realised that it would have more purpose if it was based on education. Many of the children opt out of school and the aim of the tournament has been to increase awareness of its value and the necessity of learning and sharing. In 2009 the work of his foundation was recognised when it received the FIFPRO Merit Award.

CHARITABLE MOKOENA

Aaron Mokoena was eleven years old when the Inkatha Freedom Party, political rivals of Nelson Mandela's ANC, sent more than 200 armed men into Boipatong, with the purpose of killing as many of the inhabitants of the ANC stronghold as they could. Forty-six people were massacred and rumours circulated that the IFP were returning to kill all the men and boys in the town. Mokoena's mother, Maria, who had taken care of seven children on her own following the death of her husband four years earlier, dressed the boys up in their sisters' clothes in an attempt to keep them safe. The massacre was just one stepping stone on the road to the ANC establishing control of the country. Fortunately the Mokoenas survived and Aaron, when just over 18, became the youngest man to play international football for South Africa.

Despite a football career that took him to Germany, Holland, Belgium and England, Mokoena never forgot his roots in Boipatong, growing up in a home in Zone 4, Block A, made of breeze blocks and corrugated tin. His mother supported the family by cleaning for a family in an adjacent town. When Mokoena started earning footballers' wages he bought her a house close by, although she never stopped working for the family. His wealth made him a target for threats and extortion in the locality. He bought his brother a taxi so that he could earn a living in the area but thieves stole the taxi and killed his brother. His children moved in with their grandmother and are supported by Mokoena.

Not content to simply look after his own family, Mokoena provided financial support for a hospice in the Vaal Triangle and owns a football team, The Birds, which plays in the Castle League. The aim of the football team is to provide an outlet for the young people and teach them discipline and respect. In 2008 he launched the Aaron Mokoena Foundation, which aims to bring sport, coaching and education to disadvantaged children. When the World Cup was held in South Africa in 2010, Mokoena was high profile as the country's captain and he utilised the platform to promote charitable work. In 2009 he was appointed an ambassador to 1 Goal, a charity promoting education for the underdeveloped world. A natural ambassador and leader, he was personally rewarded in 2010 when he received the Freedom of the City of London. He was the second South African to receive this honour the other being Nelson Mandela.

OTHER CHARITABLE ROVERS

Many of the players who have played for the club have formed their own charitable trusts to support those in need, among them being El Hadji Diouf, Craig Bellamy, Roque Santa Cruz and David Dunn. Jason Roberts was awarded the MBE because of his work with the charity he established to help youngsters in Grenada and in the underprivileged areas of London. A young trainee with the club, Mo Keita, who had left Africa to live in Germany when he was young, sent a huge proportion of his salary to help the youngsters in the village in the Ivory Coast where he grew up.

DID YOU KNOW?

Alan Shearer was awarded the OBE for services to football and Mike England the MBE for services to Welsh football. Jason Roberts also has an MBE for his charitable work. A player of the early years, John Rutherford, was knighted, although that was for political services. Ryan Nelsen was made an Officer of the New Zealand Order of Merit in the 2011 New Year's honours list.

The father of Stig-Inge Bjørnebye competed at the Winter Olympics of 1968 and 1972, in the ski jump.

Having never had a Portuguese player in their 137-year history, the club signed four in a month, the well-known striker Nuño Gómes and youngsters Fábio Nunes, Paulo Jorge and Edinho Junior.

In 1880 no fewer than ten Rovers players also played in the first team for the town's major cricket club, East Lancashire.

HANGING UP THE BOOTS

A modern phenomenon of sport has been the manner in which retired sportsmen have a window of opportunity to capitalise on their reputation and earn from television and radio work. Football punditry has been the most obvious outlet for the talents of some and Alan Shearer, on *Match of the Day*, has been the most successful of the old Rovers players, though Jim Beglin has also carved out a career as a expert commentator. Robbie Savage, Jason Roberts and Kevin Gallacher are also carving out roles in punditry.

In addition reality television has afforded some the opportunity to participate in areas where they are not recognised experts. With their much-lauded scientific training footballers ought to have an aptitude for dancing contests, although after the experiences of former Rovers players the jury might be still out on this theory. In 2009 Graeme Le Saux was the first man voted off *Dancing on Ice*. Since then Robbie Savage in *Strictly Come Dancing* and Lars Bohinen in the Norwegian equivalent, *Shall We Dance*, have proved more able, but without ultimate success.

Increasingly the occupations of retired players have become varied and few now follow the customary path into the licensed trade. Norman Bell, after a spell selling furniture made of porcelain, worked for the council with young offenders in the Blackburn area. This unusual combination was almost mirrored by Ben Arentoft, who worked as an art dealer and became head of the juvenile probation service in Copenhagen

Paul Shepstone opened, with his wife, a specialist lingerie shop in Leamington, while Tim Sherwood and Garry Flitcroft once launched a lifestyle magazine, aimed at WAGs. Gordon Taylor, the son of a trade union official, became secretary of the PFA in 1981 and still is in charge of the association. Simon Barker attended university after his playing days were over and then joined the PFA, where he has held various important offices.

By far the most financially successful of the old Rovers players has been Dave Whelan, who started with a corner shop, built up a chain of supermarkets which he sold to the Morrison group and became a millionaire. He invested part of the sale proceeds in JJB Sports which he floated on the stock exchange. This expanded his wealth exponentially and he was soon figuring in the *Sunday Times'* UK Rich List. He also started investing in sport and at one time owned Wigan Athletic, the famous Wigan rugby league club and Orrell rugby union club. He later divested himself of the latter two but retained control of Wigan Athletic, whose ascent to the Premier League he masterminded.

Wattie Aitkenhead became the director of a Blackburn cotton mill, although his route to the helm was greatly aided by the fact that he married the owner's daughter.

Derek Dougan became chairman and chief executive of Wolverhampton Wanderers.

The scarcity of trams makes tram driving an unusual profession but two old players, Fergus Aitken and Andy McEvoy, became drivers after they left the club. Pat Hilton worked on the construction of the Channel Tunnel.

GOALSCORERS

All players who have scored more than 60 goals

	Goals	Appearances
Simon Garner	192	528 + 37
Tommy Briggs	143	204
Alan Shearer	130	165 + 6
Ted Harper	122	177
Jack Southworth	122	133
Jack Bruton	115	344
Bryan Douglas	115	502 + 1
Eddie Latheron	104	283
Peter Dobing	104	205
Andy McEvoy	103	213
Wattie Aitkenhead	96	239
Eddie Quigley	95	166
Sid Puddefoot	87	277
Ernie Thompson	84	179
Eddie Crossan	74	302
Fred Pickering	74	158
Percy Dawson	73	151
Billy Davies	70	143
Danny Shea	65	105
John Byrom	64	146 + 3
Don Martin	63	244 + 7

THE LURE OF THE MERSEYSIDE DOLLAR

In 1888 the Rovers lost a future international, Edgar Chadwick, to Everton because they were not willing to substantially raise his pay of 10s per week. William Henry Whitehead, who was on the same pay, left for the same reason at the time and was able to get 25s at Colne (although not for long). Five years later another international forward, Jack Southworth, was offered substantially higher wages and joined Everton. It forced the Rovers' committee to publish his pay to date, which had been:

1887/88	£1 per week	£35 0s 0d
1888/89	£1 per week	£35 0s 0d
1889/90	£1 per week + £20 bonus	£55 0s 0d
1890/91	£2 per week (season), then 10s per week (summer)	£78 10s 0d
1891/92	As above + £100 bonus	£178 10s 0d
1892/93	£2 per week (season), then 10s per week (summer)	£78 10s 0d
Total		£460 10s 0d

At the time Southworth was the greatest goalscorer in football. His pay with the Rovers had been substantially more than he had been receiving at Higher Walton, which was half a crown a week. The average wage at the time was about £1 5s.

MOST APPEARANCES

	Appearances	Debut	Final Game	Birthplace
Derek Fazackerley	671 + 3	23/2/1971	26/12/1986	Preston
Ronnie Clayton	663 + 2	25/4/1951	30/4/1969	Preston
Bob Crompton	576	10/4/1897	23/2/1920	Blackburn
Simon Garner	528 + 37	29/8/1978	21/3/1992	Boston
Bryan Douglas	502 + 1	4/9/1954	5/4/1969	Blackburn
Bill Eckersley	432	1/5/1948	31/8/1960	Southport
Bill Bradshaw	426	12/9/1903	28/2/1920	Padiham
Stuart Metcalfe	421 + 13	27/4/1968	9/4/1983	Blackburn
Glenn Keeley	412 + 6	28/8/1976	9/5/1987	Barking
Colin Hendry	399 + 9	14/3/1987	10/5/1998	Keith
Harry Healless	397	14/9/1918	31/12/1932	Blackburn
Tony Parkes	387 + 5	5/9/1970	21/2/1981	Sheffield
Brad Friedel	357	18/11/2000	13/5/2008	Lakewood, Ohio, USA
Keith Newton	357	19/9/1960	13/12/1969	Manchester

	Appearances	Debut	Final Game	Birthplace
Noel Brotherston	355 + 12	20/8/1977	7/3/1987	Dundonald
Bob Pryde	345	21/10/1933	23/4/1949	Methil
Jack Bruton	344	7/12/1929	27/8/1938	Westhoughton
Terry Gennoe	334	29/8/1981	25/8/1990	Shrewsbury
Jim Branagan	333 + 4	27/10/1979	11/4/1987	Barton
Eric Bell	333	1/9/1945	29/9/1956	Bedlington
Mick McGrath	312	28/4/1956	6/11/1965	Dublin
Matt Woods	307	24/11/1956	20/5/1963	Burscough
Arthur Cowell	306	23/9/1905	13/12/1919	Blackburn
Mike Rathbone	303 + 3	10/3/1979	28/2/1987	Birmingham
Albert Walmsley	301	26/10/1907	14/2/1920	Blackburn

FACIAL AND OTHER ADORNMENTS

The first Rover to sport an earring was the Swedish international, Martin Dahlin. The only one to employ the dubious advantage of a nasal dilator (nose strip) was the Turk, Hakan Unsal. Simon Vukcevic was the first to wear a protective mask, which did not prevent him from scoring, with a header. Moustaches have been common, but Bob Crompton's under-nose appendage was an iconic image throughout football. With his retirement the moustache faded from the Ewood scene, Frank Crawley in 1923 being the last to sport one, and there was a gap of almost a quarter of a century until Harold Stephan turned up at Ewood after the war with a pencil moustache. Beards only appeared much later and it is possible that the Irish inside forward, Eamonn Rogers, was the first to try this fashion statement. The owner of the first tattoo is unknown, some of the players who served in the war would undoubtedly have obtained one, but no player has made his body into a portable art gallery in the fashion of Leon Best. Starting with 'Mum' on his chest, he also has 'Sky's the limit' and 'It's all a dream' but the most evocative, on his left arm, is the motto 'Work like a slave, eat like a king'.

DIRECTORS

When the club was converted into a limited company in 1897, three of the ten original directors were former players, including John Lewis and Richard Birtwistle, who played in the club's first fixture. The other was John Forbes who came down from Scotland in 1888 to play for the club. Lewis resigned a year later, blaming lack of public support for his decision, although he remained a shareholder who made life difficult for the directors at many an annual general meeting. Dick Birtwistle served until 1906, deciding to terminate his chairmanship after a few years of disputes about the training and tactics of the team that led to the dismissal of several trainers. Even after leaving the board he continued to act as a guarantor for the club's debts. Forbes remained a director until his death in 1928.

Two other players who first played for the Rovers before the Football League was formed became directors. Arthur Birtwistle was elected in 1903, on the nomination of John Lewis who voiced his dissatisfaction with the board. He served until 1908. Jim Forrest was elected in 1906 and served until his death in 1926. Only two other former first team players have been directors, Harry Garstang, who served from 1904 to 1925, although he lost his position for a year in 1905 and the incomparable Robert Crompton, who was elected in 1921 and lost his seat in 1931. Garstang made one appearance for the Rovers, Crompton 576. A former reserve player, Walter Tempest, was a director from 1925 until his death in 1941. He was the last former player to serve as a director.

TRAINERS

The position of trainer is now outdated but was at one time an important one. The Rovers discovered early in their existence that someone is needed to ensure the players keep fit. Three years after they were formed, their founder, John Lewis, left the club because some of the players were not keen on training (or playing) in bad weather. He soon returned and it was accepted that a committee member (normally Lewis) would supervise the team. As he became more tied up in his refereeing career, Dick Birtwistle assumed the role. With Birtwistle growing older and more occupied by business, the club finally hired a man to act as groundsman and trainer. He was Ted Murray, a local man who had been an army sergeant. The arrangement worked so admirably that the club won the FA Cup two years in succession. The committee failed to see Murray's importance, however, and when he received a better offer from Northwich, he took it. Eventually he was replaced by the old England international, Jack Hunter, who had transformed the Olympic from a rag-bag of working-class players to English FA Cup winners. With a lifetime's experience in the game, Hunter was an ideal choice, but his view of his role was at odds with that of the committee and in particular, Dick Birtwistle. He saw the trainer as a man to simply keep the team at peak fitness, but inevitably the players started to look to Hunter for advice on tactics and strategy. When New Brighton offered him more money in 1897, he reluctantly left since he knew that his current situation was not going to improve. The committee seized the chance to return to their original plan and brought in a time-served army sergeant, Tom Trimmer, a Brighton man who had married a lady from Preston when he was stationed at Fulwood Barracks. It was a brief and unsuccessful appointment and Hunter soon returned, although the club appointed their old player, Nat Walton, as his deputy.

The polemics resumed and Hunter was demoted for not keeping the directors informed but it changed little. Walton was also an experienced player who had played for England and the players once again tended to look for guidance to the trainer rather than the directors. Walton was dismissed and another army sergeant, John McKenzie, was brought in. This was another ill-fated attempt to keep power away from the trainer and even Dick Birtwistle admitted at the annual general meeting that McKenzie was not liked by the players. When Birtwistle stood down, the new chairman, Laurence Cotton, had seen enough and the old Preston full-back, Bob Holmes, was brought in. After he retired he had considerable experience coaching and training and he was an ideal choice.

Seven years later the club won the championship, and Holmes played a large part in the success. However, by the time they repeated the feat two years later, Holmes was gone, nudged quietly aside in a move that displayed that Cotton was both shrewd and ruthless. The club had appointed a former reserve player, Moy Atherton, as Holmes' assistant. He studied fitness and new techniques and his aptitude was such that Cotton was reluctant to lose him, so he gave him his head. He was a man years ahead in his field, who invented the screw-in rubber stud, that years later made Umbro and Adidas a fortune. Atherton gained no reward – he sought business advice from Bob Crompton who was of the opinion that the cost of patenting his studs would outweigh any rewards.

Atherton served from 1913 to 1933 when he was suddenly informed, without explanation, that he was no longer required. His successor, the old international full back, Arthur Cowell, received the same fate four years later. This time the reason for change was that the old Welsh international goalkeeper, Len Evans, had displayed outstanding ability in mastering the requirements of training footballers and he proved to be every bit as good as his backers had said. He did not return after the Second War when the club appointed the Arsenal and England full-back, Eddie Hapgood, as their manager. He brought with him his old Arsenal team-mate, Horace Cope. When Hapgood left, Cope also went and in 1949 Jack Weddle, who had come to the club as a player in 1938 and was made trainer to the reserves after the war, was promoted.

By this time the role had been reduced to looking after the fitness of the players, with coaches employed to provide technical help for the playing staff. A much-loved man, popular with players and spectators, he remained in the position until he retired in 1961. Jimmy Gordon, the old

Middlesbrough player, was an ideal replacement, although his role was somewhat wider as he was officially trainer-coach. He might well have become as much part of the Rovers' story as Weddle, if eight years later he had not been induced to go to Derby County by Brian Clough. Brian Birch, an ex-Manchester United player, was promoted to replace him but he quickly succumbed to the offer of overseas riches and joined Galatasaray. Replacing him was the old Crystal Palace forward, Arthur Proudler, who was the last trainer-coach. When he left, the function of trainer disappeared, becoming obsolete in a sport where the coach and masseur provided all the services necessary.

MANAGERS

The position of manager did not exist in the pre-war years but functionally the club secretary reformed this role.

	From –To	Job description
Thomas Mitchell	1884 – Oct 1896	Secretary
Joseph Walmsley	1896 – May 1903	Secretary
Robert B. Middleton	Jul 1903 – Sep 1925	Secretary
Jack Carr	Feb 1922 – Oct 1925	Manager
	Oct 1925 – Dec 1926	Secretary-manager
Bob Crompton	Dec 1926 – Feb 1931	Honorary manager
Arthur Barritt	Mar 1931 – Mar 1936	Secretary-manager
Reg Taylor	Oct 1936 – May 1938	Secretary-manager

	From – To	Job description
Bob Crompton	May 1938 – Mar 1941	Manager
Reg Taylor	Mar 1941 – Jan 1946	Secretary-manager
Eddie Hapgood	Jan 1946 – Feb 1947	Manager
Will Scott	Apr 1947 – Dec 1947	
Jack Bruton	Dec 1947 – May 1949	
Jackie Bestall	Jun 1949 – May 1953	
Johnny Carey	Jun 1953 – Oct 1958	
Dally Duncan	Oct 1958 – Jun 1960	
Jack Marshall	Sep 1960 – Feb 1967	
Eddie Quigley	Feb 1967 – Apr 1967	Caretaker manager
	Apr 1967 – Oct 1970	
Johnny Carey	Oct 1970 – Jun 1971	
Ken Furphy	Jul 1971 – Dec 1973	
Gordon Lee	Jan 1974 – Jun 1975	
Jim Smith	Jun 1975 – Mar 1978	
Jim Iley	Apr 1978 – Oct 1978	
John Pickering	Oct 1978 – Feb 1979	Caretaker manager
	Feb 1979 – May 1979	
Howard Kendall	Jun 1979 – Jun 1981	
Bobby Saxton	Jun 1981 – Dec 1986	
Tony Parkes	Dec 1986 – Feb 1987	Caretaker manager
Don Mackay	Feb 1987 – Sep 1991	
Tony Parkes	Sep 1991 – Oct 1991	Caretaker manager
Kenny Dalglish	Oct 1991 – Jun 1995	
Ray Harford	Jun 1995 – Oct 1996	

	From – To	Job description
Tony Parkes	Oct 1996 – Jul 1997	Caretaker manager
Roy Hodgson	Jul 1997 – Nov 1998	
Tony Parkes	Nov 1998 – Dec 1998	Caretaker manager
Brian Kidd	Dec 1998 – Nov 1999	
Tony Parkes	Nov 1999 – Dec 1999	Caretaker manager
	Dec 1999 – Mar 2000	
Graeme Souness	Mar 2000 – Sep 2005	
Mark Hughes	Sep 2005 – Jun 2008	
Paul Ince	Jun 2008 – Dec 2008	
Sam Allardyce	Dec 2008 – Dec 2010	
Steve Kean	Dec 2010 –	

DID I REALLY SAY THAT?

'Everybody is thinking we as directors ought to find a lot of money but I am one who is not digging in my pocket. If any team comes for any player they can take him tomorrow if the price is right.'

The alleged words of W.H. Grimshaw in 1933, according to a future director, Arthur Tempest. Grimshaw denied having said them

'The board are not yet of the opinion that floodlit football is going to last.'

Spoken by the club chairman, Tom Blackshaw, in 1955

THERE'S ONLY ONE BLACKBURN ROVERS

Actually there are two top-class sides called Blackburn Rovers. A team of that name was formed in 1965 and play at the Buffalo City Stadium in East London, Eastern Cape, South Africa. In 2010 they were promoted to the National First Division.

There was also a Grimsby trawler named *Blackburn Rovers*. Commissioned in 1934 by Consolidated Fisheries it was requisitioned by the Admiralty for use on anti-submarine duties. On 2 June 1940 it sank during the Dunkirk evacuation.

A musical work, 'The Football Polka', was dedicated to the all-conquering Rovers side of the early 1880s. The composer was A.B. Bentley, brother of the famed football administrator J.J. Bentley.

ALL-TIME TEAM

Every fan can select his or her fantasy XI. Having watched the Rovers for over sixty years, here is my selection, based on players I have seen. The only postwar player I never saw who warranted inclusion would probably be Bob Pryde.

Goalkeeper – Brad Friedel. This was probably the easiest choice, simply because of the manner in which incredible saves became routine. No other goalkeeper has ever possessed Friedel's ability to present a huge target in protecting the goal. Many goalkeepers use their legs well in one-on-one situations but Friedel stopped a huge number of shots because of his ability to use his entire body in reflex situations. The other goalkeepers under consideration were Roger Jones, who brought new levels of goalkeeping excellence to the club and the greatly underrated Jim Arnold, who made fewer mistakes than any goalkeeper I have seen.

Right-back – Keith Newton. In the end the choices were reduced to two, Newton and Henning Berg. Newton was a tremendously athletic force of nature who had the ability to have played anywhere. His tackling was razor sharp, he competed powerfully in the air but it was his sheer power as a surging force from the back that made him a great player. I have never seen a better stand-up tackler than Berg, a man with such balance and composure that he could miss with one foot but recover and tackle with the other.

Centre-backs – Henning Berg and Mike England. Five players were on my shortlist, the others being Colin Hendry, Chris Samba and Matt Woods. In the end the decision was surprisingly easy. Berg is technically the best defender I have ever seen. A highly competitive player, he had a thorough knowledge of angles, body momentum and positioning that turned a demanding physical position into a science. Mike England was simply a phenomenon, another player who could have played anywhere, a silky, natural footballer who had the physique to handle the position but whose ability on the ball added another dimension to the team. Samba has the innate potential to be the best of all, although he will be hard pushed to rival the selected players. In my opinion Hendry was over-rated because of the qualities that made him a cult hero. Although a dominating, inspirational figure he was also a man who it was difficult to play alongside, and several good players struggled to fit in with him. Matt Woods is a player who history has not treated kindly. He was an immense figure who should have gained international honours when he was the best centre-half in the country, when Billy Wright was winding down his England career.

Left-back – Bill Eckersley. This was a straight choice between Eckersley and Graeme Le Saux, two players who were remarkably similar in style. Eckersley had a better temperament, was never ruffled and played with greater consistency.

Centre midfield – Ronnie Clayton and Tugay. When looking at the midfield positions the situation became complicated because of the versatility of players and the requirements of different systems. Undoubtedly the best playmaker the club has ever had was Bryan Douglas who, in the old inside left position, created goals through sheer genius. However he was also a mesmeric right winger, where he received his international caps, and because the next best right-sided midfield player was some way behind in quality, it made sense to select him there. This created the opportunity to include Tugay, a man whose mastery of the ball was unique. The natural choice for the more defensive central midfield role was Ronnie Clayton, who was a magnificent athlete, who could run all day and had near perfect timing so that his tackling was always judged to a tee. He was also strong enough in the air to have been considered as a central defender. Under consideration for this role was David Batty, who was also the perfect player to orchestrate ball possession. In the more forward role an alternative to Tugay was Roy Vernon, a smooth, stylish player who could also shoot with venom.

Right midfield – Bryan Douglas. (See above)

Left midfield – Damien Duff. This was another simple choice because Duff is as complete a left winger as any in the game. His main rival was Bobby Langton, a direct, uncomplicated player who also could score goals. Mention should also be made of Dave Wagstaffe who had some feints and tricks that belonged on the stage.

Strikers – Alan Shearer and Andy McEvoy. No explanation is required for the inclusion of Shearer but it is probable that few will remember just how good a striker McEvoy was. Only Jimmy Greaves surpassed him in his ability to ghost off the shoulder of the last defender and then stroke the ball past the goalkeeper with cool precision. The only other player under consideration was Fred Pickering, who had much of Shearer's physical presence. Mention must also be made of Mike Newell, who was not as prolific as the aforementioned trio but had few equals as a hard-working team player.